March of the Moun

North-West Mounted Police patrol at Fort Walsh in 1878. The red and white pennons carried by the men are the same as those used today in the RCMP's world-famous musical ride.

FRONT COVER
Our thanks to the Public Archives of Canada and the C.W. Jefferys' Estate for permission to reprint C.W. Jefferys' painting, "March to the Rockies of the North-West Mounted Police, 1874."

BACK COVER
NWMP Sergeant on patrol. Despite handicaps such as single-shot rifles in contrast to the whisky traders' repeating Winchesters, the Mounties quickly established law and order throughout a lawless land. Illustration courtesy RCMP.

PHOTO CREDITS
Glenbow-Alberta Institute: 7 (bottom), 38 (top), 41, 46, 48-49, 52 (top), 58, 71 (top), 74 (top), 84, 95, 98-99, 100, 103 (inset), 108, 113 (top), 119, 126, 142 (top), 149 (top), 155; Heritage House: 44, 54, 78 (bottom two), 149 (bottom); Manitoba Archives: 15, 68; Notman Archives: 20; Provincial Archives of Alberta: 62, 74-75, 89 (bottom), 113 (bottom); Public Archives of Canada: 11, 28-29, 36, 71 (bottom), 82, 136 (top), 144; RCMP: Title page, 7 (top), 13, 38 (bottom), 52 (bottom), 75 (top), 78 (top), 103, 111, 124, 128-129, 142 (bottom), 157; Saskatchewan Government: 9, 136 (bottom), 137.

CANADIAN CATALOGUING IN PUBLICATION DATA
Denny, Cecil E., Sir, 1850-1928.
March of the Mounties

ISBN 1-895811-06-6

1. North West Mounted Police (Canada) — History.
2. Canada, Western — History. I TItle.
FC3216.4.D45 1994 971.2'02 C93-091725-1
F1060.9.D45 1994

First Edition - 1994

HERITAGE HOUSE PUBLISHING COMPANY LTD.
Unit #8 17921 55th Ave., Surrey, B.C. V3S 6C4

Printed in Canada

The Author

Sir Cecil Edward Denny was born in England on December 14, 1850. He was the second son of the Reverend Robert Day Denny and the half-brother of Sir Arthur Denny. He inherited the title on his half-brother's death in February 1922.

At 19 he emigrated to the United States and farmed on land that is now a suburb of Chicago, Illinois. In February 1874, Denny obtained a commission as Captain in the North-West Mounted Police, one of the first 300 officers, non-commissioned officers, and men in the force. In the winter of 1874-5 he assisted in constructing Fort Macleod, and in August 1875 was in charge of the detachment that built Fort Calgary.

Captain Denny resigned from the Mounted Police in 1882 after eight years to become Indian Agent for the Cree, Assiniboine and Blackfoot. For several years he was in charge of the tribes and was made an honorary chief. His title, Chief "Beaver Coat," derived from his wearing a beaver overcoat. He later resigned when the government broke its promise to the Indians.

Denny was ranching near Fort Macleod in 1885 when the Riel, or North-West, Rebellion broke out. He was requested by Prime Minister John A. Macdonald to take charge of the western plains Indians. At the close of the rebellion, he received the thanks of the Canadian Government for his efforts in preventing them from going on the warpath. After the rebellion, Denny returned to his ranch and did special scout work for the police.

He later went to British Columbia. Here he remained for two years as Police Magistrate at Fort Steele during construction of the Crow's Nest Pass Railway in the 1890s.

Denny occupied many other positions in government service, including being in charge of the North-West Mounted Police pack-train on the Peace River exploration expedition from 1904 to 1906. From 1922 to 1927, he was Archivist for the Province of Alberta, and assisted in the Provincial Library in Edmonton. He was the author of numerous magazine and newspaper articles relating to Western Canada and Western life, and was also the author of two notable books, both out of print. They are *The Riders of the Plains* and *The Law Marches West,* from which this book is excerpted.

Following a long illness, he died August 24, 1928, at 78. He was accorded a public funeral in Calgary and buried in the Mounted Police plot in the city which he had helped to establish over 50 years before.

CONTENTS

Introduction

In the early 1870s the 1,000-mile region between Winnipeg and the Rocky Mountains was a lawless wilderness. In what is today southern Alberta, upwards of 500 whisky peddlers from the U.S. were wiping out the Indians with bullets and liquor. They had even established a series of forts, with one of them, Whoop-up near today's Lethbridge, complete with cannon.

The problem began in 1869 when the fledgling Dominion of Canada agreed to give the Hudson's Bay Company some $1.5 million and land grants to relinquish its rights to Rupert's Land and its trading monopoly in what was then called The North-Western Territory. In return, the Dominion gained control of a region from which evolved much of today's Quebec and Ontario, all of Manitoba, Saskatchewan and Alberta, and the Yukon and Northwest Territories. To maintain order, Prime Minister Sir John A. Macdonald decided to form a mounted police force. Unfortunately, these plans were dropped and a region rivalling in size the United States became a land of no law.

In the previous 200 years a semblance of order had been maintained by the Hudson's Bay Company. Under its jurisdiction, Chief Factors were given powers to try criminal cases and an endeavor was made to preserve law and order for the benefit of profit and loss.

But with transfer from Hudson's Bay control a new element was tragically introduced into the Indian way of life — unlimited liquor. Not that the HBC and other traders were teetotallers in their transactions with Indians. But they did exercise control on the sensible premise that drunken Indians made poor trappers and were unpredictable and very dangerous. In 1804 Alexander Henry, a trader for the North West Company at Pembina, noted in his journal: "Indians having asked for liquor and promised to decamp and hunt well all summer, I gave them some. Grand Gueule stabbed Capot Rouge, Le Boeuf stabbed his young wife in the arm, Little Shell almost beat his old mother's brains out with a club, and there was terrible fighting among them. I sowed garden seeds."

But not all traders peacefully sowed their seeds during the Indians' brawls. Some became the victims, their bodies lying in lonely graves. It was obvious to the businessmen of the Hudson's Bay Company that dead traders or dead Indians made them no profit. Hence they strove to have the Indians' way of life disturbed as little as possible, even to actively discouraging any settlement of their vast domain.

In the late 1860s, however, a dramatic change occurred in the form of aggressive Yankees from Montana Territory. The

U.S. Civil War was now history and covered wagons rumbled across the plains carrying settlers to California, Oregon and other western regions. Among new communities to appear was Fort Benton on the Upper Missouri River about 100 miles south of what would one day be Alberta.

Fort Benton became the supply area for a massive region of the U.S. plains and unprincipled "free traders" who ventured north to challenge the HBC trading monopoly. Their main stock-in-trade was whisky. Without concern for its catastrophic consequences they dispensed it from trading posts, or forts as they called them, with colorful names such as Whisky Gap, Robber's Roost, Fort Slide Out, Fort Stand Off, Spitzee Post and Fort Whoop-up. The latter became the focal point of the liquor traffic.

It was born in 1869 when John Jerome Healy and Alfred B. Hamilton, two U.S. traders from Fort Benton, built 11 log cabins at the junction of the St. Mary and Oldman Rivers. They surrounded the cabins with a flimsy palisade and that winter netted $50,000. Unfortunately, the Indians set fire to it, feeling that they were being cheated — an assessment that was undoubtedly correct.

Hamilton and Healy, however, weren't about to leave so lucrative a land. They started another fort a few hundred feet away — one that wouldn't burn so easily. It was built of heavy, squared timbers with a sturdy palisade loopholed for rifles and two bastions complete with cannon. On one of the bastions was a flagpole from which fluttered Healy's personal flag — blue and red — which at a distance resembled the Stars and Stripes. The fort also had a bell like that on a locomotive which was rung when trading was to start.

The interior contained cookhouse, blacksmith shop, stables and living quarters with huge stone fireplaces. All windows were barred, as were the chimneys, since in their craving for whisky Indians had broken into trading posts by dropping down the chimney. The post, called Fort Hamilton (but soon to be known as "Whoop-up"), took 30 men two years to build and cost some $25,000.

Indians were seldom permitted inside the palisade. They pushed their buffalo hides and other items through a small wicket near the main gate and exchanged them for blankets, guns, and whisky — particularly whisky. When the furs were gone and the whisky too, they traded not only the horses they needed to hunt the buffalo on which they survived, but their wives and even daughters as young as twelve.

"The firey [fiery] water flowed as freely as the streams running from the rocky Mountains," wrote a Catholic missionary, "and hundreds of poor Indians fell victims to the white

Fort Whoop-up, shown in the 1870s, was built in what is now southern Alberta by U.S. whisky traders Alfred Hamilton and John Healy. It was sturdily built of squared cottonwood logs and had its own flag and a cannon. Its purpose? To protect U.S. traders who, in exchange for a concoction called whisky, virtually robbed the Indians of their horses, furs, women and even their lives.

man's craving for money, some poisoned, some frozen to death whilst in a state of intoxication, and many shot down by American bullets."

The Reverend John McDougall, one of the West's renowned missionaries, noted: "Scores of thousands of buffalo robes and hundreds of thousands of wolf and fox skins and most of the best horses the Indians had were taken south into Montana, and the chief article of barter for these was alcohol. In this traffic very many Indians were killed, and also quite a number of white men. Within a few miles of us ... forty-two able-bodied men were the victims among themselves, all slain in the drunken rows. These were Blackfoot.... There was no law but might. Some terrible scenes occurred when whole camps went on the spree, as was frequently the case, shooting, stabbing, killing, freezing, dying.

"Thus these atrocious debauches were continuing all that winter not far from us. Mothers lost their children. These were either frozen to death or devoured by the myriad dogs of the camp. The birth-rate decreased and the poor red man was in a fair way towards extinction, just because some men, coming out of Christian countries, and themselves the evolution of Christian civilization, were now ruled by lust and greed."

In May 1873 the Canadian Parliament had passed a bill providing for the establishment of a "Police Force in the North-West Territories," and for magistrates, courts and jails. But a surprise obstacle was Prime Minister Sir John A. Macdonald. Not that he opposed the force. In fact he had been the primary motivation behind the legislation. But Macdonald was a marvelous procrastinator, so accomplished that he earned the nickname "Old Tomorrow." Now he put off implementing the legislation.

A remarkable contrast to this lack of action and consequent rule "by lust and greed" was the province of British Columbia across the Rocky Mountains. It was born in 1858 when gold was discovered on the Fraser River. At the time there were only a few hundred whites in a region as big as Washington, Oregon and California combined. This far-flung wilderness was essentially a Hudson's Bay Company fur preserve, the only dots in the wilderness a few Company forts. Into this region surged some 30,000 men with gold in their eyes.

Most were from the U.S., virtually all heavily armed. In June 1858 one writer noted that they "...were all equipped with the universal revolver, many of them carrying a brace of such, as well as a bowie knife." Another observer, English author Kinahan Cornwallis, wrote of one that, "He carried a couple of revolvers, and a bowie knife, with the point of which he took

Farwell Post, near today's Fort Walsh National Historic Park, was rebuilt by the RCMP in 1967. The original building burned down the day after the Cypress Hills Massacre in 1873. The Post has been refurbished to the 1873 period, below, and features guides in period costume. During the restoration, the RCMP uncovered the skeleton of Ed Legrace, a whisky trader killed during the massacre and buried under the floor.

the opportunity of picking his teeth immediately after supper."

By November, however, a police force with judges had been formed and carrying the "belt gun" was banned. Even though there were fewer than three dozen lawmen, they kept the peace. One reason was that the miners soon realized that justice would prevail — even if a judge had to ride horseback three weeks to reach his log courthouse.

As Judge Peter O'Reilly told a group of miners in eastern B.C. when he arrived: "Boys, I am here to keep order and to administer the law. Those who don't want law and order can git, but those who stay with the camp, remember on what side of the Line the camp is; for boys, if there is shooting in Kootenay there will be hanging in Kootenay."

The result of this clearly stated policy was summarized by Pacific Northwest historian Hubert Howe Bancroft: "Never in the pacification and settlement of any section of America have there been so few disturbances, so few crimes against life and property."

By contrast, in the North-West Territories, the do nothing policy of "Old Tomorrow" resulted in yet another slaughter.

The Cypress Hills, which straddle the southern border of what is today Alberta-Saskatchewan, had for centuries been a favorite Indian region. Its miles of jackpine made excellent tipi poles and it was rich in buffalo, black and grizzly bear, deer and other wildlife.

The white men found it equally attractive, especially the whisky traders. Among them were Abel Farwell and Moses Solomon who built whisky forts side by side deep in the Hills. In May 1873 a band of Assiniboine were camped near Farwell's post and, as later reported, "...whisky flowed like water ... and by mid-day the tribesmen were all hopelessly drunk...."

Probably nothing extraordinary would have happened but for the arrival of a party of wolfers — men who lived by poisoning wolves then selling the hides. Wolfers were disliked by the Indians because their dogs were often among the poison victims. For their part these wolfers — later described as "...persons of the worst class in the country" — had no concern for either the dogs or the Indians they killed.

About noon on June 1 a man named Hammond who was staying at Farwell's post discovered that his horse was missing. He accused the Assiniboine and vowed to take two of theirs in retaliation. When he asked the wolfers to help, they eagerly grabbed their rifles and six-guns.

Who fired the first shot is uncertain, as is the number of Assiniboine men, women and children killed. Best estimates are that the wolfers massacred at least 20 Indians, including

Prime Minister Sir John A. Macdonald, "Old Tomorrow," in the early 1870s.

Chief Little Soldier. He was roused from a drunken stupor by his wife who attempted to lead him to safety in the woods. He refused to go, and as he stood defenceless was murdered by one of the wolfers. Another Indian, an old man, was killed with a hatchet, his head severed then mounted on a lodge pole. Four women were taken to Solomon's post, among them Little Chief's wife. Here she and another young woman were repeatedly raped. Next morning the wolfers buried their only casualty, Ed Legrace, under the floor of Farwell's post, burned it and Solomon's, then hurriedly left.

News of the slaughter was three months reaching Ottawa and even then came via U.S. authorities. While there was indignation over the fact that "...defenceless Canadian Indian women and children had been murdered by the U.S. renegades...." Macdonald still held back his recruiting schedule. Then on September 20 he received a telegram from Lieutenant-Governor Morris of the North-West Territories: "What have you done as to Police Force? Their absence may lead to grave disaster."

This time, after four years of stalling, "Old Tomorrow" finally acted.

Art Downs
Surrey, B.C.

CHAPTER ONE

Policemen for the Lawless Land

Of 300 recruits in the new North-West Mounted Police, only two were experienced lawmen and not many more could ride a horse.

The Bill which had been passed by Parliament in May 1873 provided for a civil force in uniform, drilled in simple movements taken from the British Cavalry Regulations, and to be conducted much upon the system of a cavalry regiment. Thus was taken the first step in the mustering of a corps, the daring and resourcefulness of which have carried its fame around the world, and brought lustre to the name of Canada — the North-West Mounted Police, known today as the Royal Canadian Mounted Police.

"Ordinarily speaking, no more wildly impossible undertaking was ever staged than the establishment of Canadian authority and Canadian law throughout the western prairies by a handful of mounted police," wrote the Honorable Frank Oliver, pioneer newspaperman and member of the Federal Cabinet. In large measure world opinion took for granted that lawlessness must accompany pioneer conditions. Canada's Mounted Police was a challenge to that idea.

The pay of the police was: Commissioner, a salary not to exceed $2,600 a year, and not less than $2,000; Superintendents, not exceeding $1,400, and not less than $1,000; Paymasters, not exceeding $900; Quartermasters, not exceeding $500; Surgeons, not exceeding $1,400, and not less than $1,000; Veterinary Surgeons, not exceeding $1,600; ordinary Constables $1.00 per day; and Sub-Constables, 75 cents a day. Looking back at the rate of pay granted the original force of Mounted Police, and the work they performed, it seems poor remuneration. But the lure of the unknown and the prospect of great adventure brought thou-

The Force's
first commander,
George A. French

The 1874 photo below is probably the earliest one taken of the NWMP. Seated is Sub-Inspector John French, later killed during the Riel Rebellion. Standing behind him is Sub-Inspector F. J. Dickens, son of author Charles Dickens, who had to abandon Fort Pitt during the North-West (Riel) Rebellion.

sands to apply when only hundreds were required.

By October three troops — A, B, and C — of 50 men each had been organized. In command was Lieutenant-Colonel George A. French who had been "loaned" to Canada by the British Government.

The first contingent was sent in the fall of 1873 by the Dawson Route to Winnipeg, Manitoba. This Route was the all-Canadian way to the West, dreaded by all who had experienced it and its reputation awing those who had never experienced it. Established by the fur traders, it was some 450 miles long and consisted mostly of lakes and rivers. There were dozens of portages, some up to two miles long, which became notable for mud in wet weather and clouds of mosquitoes during the summer. The recruits, however, passed their first test like veteran voyageurs. When they arrived at the fur trading post, the *Winnipeg Manitoban* reported: "Judging from the first detachment, the Mounted Police are a fine body of men."

From Winnipeg the men were sent some 20 miles north to Lower Fort Garry, an old Hudson's Bay Company trading post. Here they remained until the following spring. Then the remainder of the force, which would be recruited during the winter in Toronto, would join them and bring all transport, supplies, etc., required for the arduous journey into the unknown West. They would also bring enough horses to provide each man with his trooper, and teams enough to move the transport.

When Lieutenant-Colonel French arrived at Fort Garry in November, he quickly realized how inadequate the 150-man force was to patrol an area larger than Europe. On his return to Ottawa he urged upon the Government the necessity of a much larger force, and on his recommendation it was increased to 300 men. The additional men became troops D, E and F.

At Fort Garry, Sergeant-Major Griesbach took charge of the disciplining and instructed the men in foot drill, while Sergeant-Major Steele took over the breaking-in of the horses, and instructed the non-commissioned officers and men in riding. The foot and mounted drill was continued in fair weather and foul, from early morning until late at night. Much weeding out of bad characters among the men was needed. The three troops were reduced in number, and were not brought up to full strength until the following spring when the remainder of the force arrived.

Much discomfort was caused the men at Fort Garry by the lack of adequate winter clothing, that forwarded from the East having been delayed until spring by the impassability of the Dawson Route. It was understood that the expedition westward would start in the spring, and the question of supplies and transport was thoroughly gone into while Commissioner

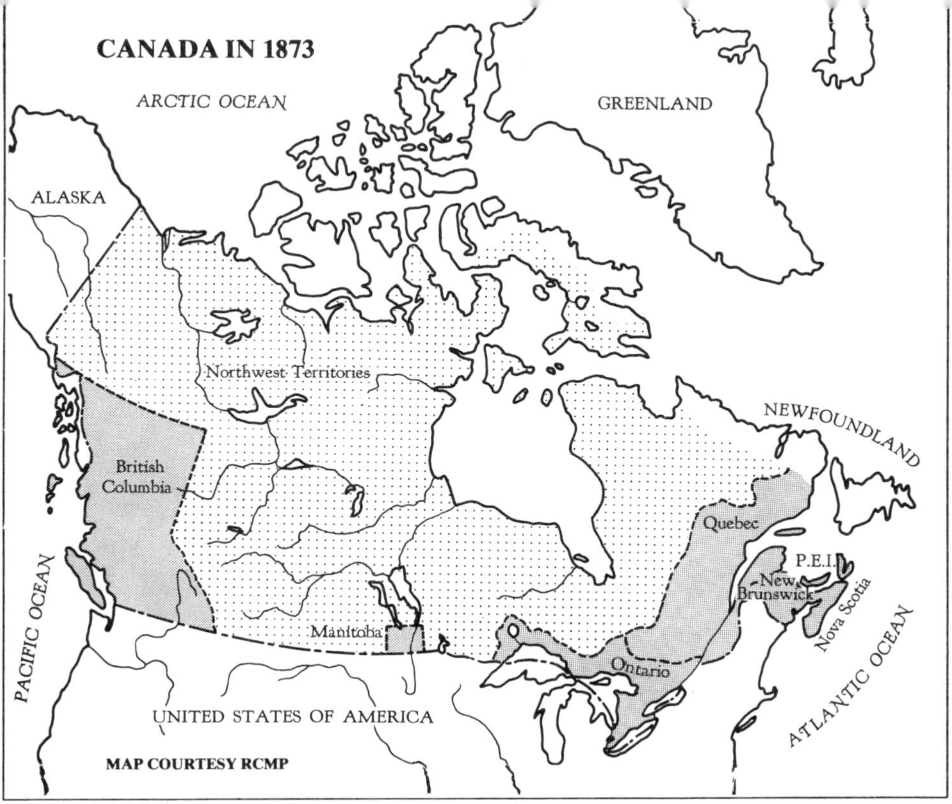

Canada in 1873, and Crow Indians killed in the Sweet Grass Hills by Piegans in 1873, the year the North-West Mounted Police was born.

French remained. On his return to Ottawa in February 1874, he recommended that stores and provisions should be transported westward by the force itself; also that cattle for slaughter should be driven along on foot, thus the need for carrying pork or pemmican in quantities be avoided.

Colonel French reports: "In the spring of 1874 arrangements had to be made for the supply of arms, ammunition, and stores of every description. Uniforms had to be designed and supplied, men enlisted, requisitions made to the Imperial Government for field guns and stores, horses to be purchased, and a tremendous amount of work done in a very short time."

In April 1874 most of the men required were assembled at Toronto, and every endeavour was made by all ranks to pick up as much instruction as possible in the limited time available for drill, riding, target practice, etc. The Regimental Sergeant-Major was an old officer of the 13th Hussars, Captain Miles. With the assistance of Sergeant Francis, a Crimean veteran, he did splendid work in drilling the recruits, both in the riding school and on foot. Practice with the nine-pound guns was carried out under the instruction of Inspector Jackson, an ex-officer from the battery at Kingston, and a gun team formed. There was much rifle practice, and as the majority had been used to arms, more or less, the instruction proceeded satisfactorily.

In the riding school things did not go so well. The recruits, for the most part, were unused to horses and many accidents occurred. As the Commissioner stated, the practice the men would have on the long march West would make of them good horsemen before its conclusion. During the preparation at Toronto, Lieutenant-Colonel French paraded the men on several occasions, and told of the hardships to be encountered on the journey westward. He also advised any who might be of faint heart to apply for discharge, which he promised to grant, but few did. The force collected at Toronto was therefore an unusually efficient one, made up of the hardiest men that could have been got together in any country. They started on an expedition at which veteran soldiers might well have faltered.

The first uniform consisted of a red tunic, black breeches with two white stripes, forage cap and helmet, high black leather boots, heavy dark blue overcoat with cape, belt with revolver and cartridge pouch, and Snider carbine. The trouser stripes were afterwards changed to red, and later again to yellow, as at present. The saddles were of the "McClellan" make. They were a poor type of saddle, with high uncomfortable cantle. The carbine in a bucket at the side was most awkward, the butt projecting over the top of the saddle, making it very difficult to mount.

They would be day after day on the march, night after night on picket or guard, working at high pressure for months from daylight until dark, and too frequently after dark. There would be little rest even on Sunday. They would ever push forward, delighted when a pure spring was met with, and still uncomplaining when salt water or the refuse of a mud hole was the only liquid available. At times they would be obliged to drink liquid which, when passed through a filter, was still the color of ink. The fact of horses and oxen dying for want of food wouldn't dishearten or stop them. Pushing on with dogged determination, they would carry through under difficulties which can only be appreciated by those who witnessed them.

The force which left Toronto in June 1874 comprised 16 officers, 201 men and 244 horses. Nine carloads of wagons and agricultural implements were attached to the trains at Sarnia, and another containing 34 horses was taken on at Detroit. The route from Toronto to Dufferin, a point in Manitoba near Pembina, North Dakota, where the three troops from Winnipeg had instructions to proceed and meet those from Toronto, was through the United States to Fargo, North Dakota, about 150 miles from Dufferin, and the terminus of the Northern Pacific Railroad.

Very little personal baggage could be taken, as the transport was limited and most of it needed to convey provisions and forage. Those involved had only a vague idea of the journey before them and the country westward to the mountains. Probably no expedition of such importance ever before undertook an 800-mile march across vast plains without competent guides, believing that at the end they would have to subdue lawless bands of desperadoes, with such complete faith in themselves and such ignorance of what they were to encounter.

On leaving Toronto we had a fairly well organized force; people all over Canada took the greatest interest in the organization and its success. The journey throughout was watched not only in Canada, but in England with lively interest. The greatest anxiety was manifested as to the fate of the little band when many months passed after its departure and no word whatever had been received of the expedition.

We were ready on Friday, June 5, 1874, to load the transport horses and baggage in two special trains that would take us without change to Fargo. The loading was accomplished after the hardest kind of work by the morning of June 6. The trains pulled out, amid adieus and good wishes, to the accompaniment of martial bands, exploding torpedoes, and encouraging cheers.

Quarters on the trains, particularly at night, were rather cramped. The horses were unloaded three times a day for feed and water, making hard work at the stops. We took meals at the different stations, arrangements having been made beforehand so that everything was ready on our arrival. Even so, sometimes our numbers taxed the accommodation of the smaller stations. We fared well, however, no pains being spared to give us the best they had. We arrived at Chicago on June 7 and put up at the stockyards, unloading the horses and feeding them in the pens during the night. A strong picket of two officers and 30 men kept guard over them. A heavy thunderstorm made it unpleasant for those on duty, with the men thoroughly soaked and tired by morning. There were few hotels near the stockyards, it was difficult to get meals, and the men who slept in the cars were glad enough to get away.

In St Paul, reached on June 10, it rained continually during our stay. Few of us had waterproofs, the uniforms being packed and the men travelling in plain clothes. The dealers in clothing had a windfall in the sale of waterproofs and overcoats to the contingent. We left next day for Fargo, our last station. It rained steadily until we arrived, when it cleared and we had beautiful weather.

Fargo was a small place consisting of a station, one or two small stores, and one hotel. We unloaded everything, and after picketing and feeding the horses, got out and began assembling the wagons. This proved a tedious business, as they came in detached parts. Eventually all cars were emptied and the contents placed on the ground so that the parts could be picked out as required. The saddlery from England was also in pieces, each box complete in itself, but it was soon sorted and put together by the saddlers. When one looked round and saw acres covered by sections of wagons and stores of all kinds, it appeared as if we should not get away for a week. But by the evening of June 14 not only were the wagons loaded, but all had pulled out and made camp some 6 miles from Fargo. A guard consisting of 26 men, with myself as officer in charge, did duty that night, this being the first real duty on the plains. We finished adjusting the loads at midnight of the 15th. The horses also were branded on the hoof with their respective numbers.

On June 16 the force moved out for Fort Dufferin, 180 miles distant, with horses in prime condition, and the men in good spirits. We travelled by troops, D supplying the advance guard, and F the rear. We made 36 miles on the first day, and camped on the bank of the Red River. On June 17 we again made a march of 36 miles.

The long marches during these first days were a mistake. Our heavily loaded wagons had much to do with animals dying subsequently on the longer and more arduous journey across the plains. The days were hot and the flies bad, but we were beginning to get hardened to the work. Our rations were scant, consisting only of biscuits and tea. On the 18th we made another 35 miles and saw the first Indian camp of Sioux, and to us who had never seen Indians, they were quite a novelty. On the 19th we camped near an American military post at Pembina on the frontier between North Dakota and Manitoba. The American officers were most hospitable, and the men did a good deal of fraternizing with the American soldiers.

We crossed over at this point into Manitoba, and reached Dufferin on June 19. Here we met the three troops from Fort Garry. They had been joined a few weeks before leaving by Lieutenant-Colonel James F. Macleod, C.M.G., who had been appointed Assistant Commissioner of the force. On meeting these three troops, several days were spent in rearranging the loads for our journey across the plains, distributing horses and wagons among the six troops, transferring men, branding the animals and getting ready generally for the 800-mile march.

On the night of June 21 a terrible thunderstorm struck our camp, accompanied by wind and hail. Nearly all the tents went down. The horses had been picketed too long, heavy lines stretched over posts. Over 200 broke loose and stampeded through the camp, overturning wagons, flattening the tents, and severely injuring several of the men. Confusion reigned. Darkness split by vivid lightning, stinging hail, and the charge of maddened horses created a pandemonium not easily forgotten. The thunder was deafening, making it almost impossible to give orders. Officers and men alike were only partly dressed, but there was no panic. Two Constables, Wilde and Francis, with three Sub-Constables — Oliver, Barton, and Sinclair — managed to secure horses and, mounting bareback, followed after the racing herd. The darkness was so dense, however, that they could see nothing and soon returned. We passed a miserable night in the open, but when morning dawned warm and bright we dried our clothes, repitched the camp, and were soon once more our cheerful selves.

Sixty men were detailed to follow the horses. After some days the majority were recovered, but 25 were never seen again. A few were found dead, while those brought back were much the worse for their wild race. Some had travelled nearly 50 miles before being picked up. We had other storms while at Dufferin, but the horses were hobbled and well guarded. There were no more stampedes.

The troops now numbered from A to F, and were composed of an Inspector, two Sub-Inspectors, and some 50 non-commissioned officers and men each. The horses and transport wagons were also divided equally among the troops. The two nine-pound guns [actually cannon which weighed about a ton each] were attached to D troop, with Sub-Inspector Jackson in charge. The horses required shoeing, which with our small portable forge, took time. Parades were held and there was much drilling. Bad whisky was easily obtainable, and several undesirable characters were discharged for drunkenness and other offences. The weather remained unsettled during our stay, making it hard for the men to get through the work. They grumbled considerably, with six or seven men deserting at Dufferin, but we were doubtless better off without them. At Dufferin came the first pay-day since leaving Toronto. It was also the last many of us saw for a year, since direct communication with Ottawa was opened only long after our march across the plains.

The baggage allowance over and above the kit was 50 pounds to each officer, and 10 pounds per man, not enough to allow transport of any luxuries. One hundred and twenty oxen and carts were purchased, and 30 half-breeds (Metis) engaged to drive them. Each carried 500 pounds of forage ration and other supplies.

For several decades the Red River cart, built entirely of wood, was the main method of transportation on the prairie. The NWMP used 114 to help haul supplies on the trek westward.

CHAPTER TWO

March of the Mounties

Challenging 800 miles of roadless prairie while herding livestock, dragging two cannon which weighed a ton each, and the prospect of "Hot Work" at Fort Whoop-up.

We were all in readiness for the start by July 6, when word came that a large band of Sioux had attacked and murdered a number of settlers at St. Joe, a small town in Dakota. The officer commanding the United States troops contacted Colonel French, asking his co-operation in cutting off these Indians should they cross into Canada. Three troops, armed and mounted, started for the point where it was supposed the Indians might enter. They returned next day, having seen no Indians.

The Sioux deeply resented the white man's intrusion into their land and were probably the most unforgiving of all Indian tribes. In 1862 from their reservations along the Upper Minnesota River they embarked on a campaign to rid the land of whites. When the uprising was finally quelled, a minimum of 450 — and possibly as many as 800 — white men, women and children had been murdered. For their part in the uprising, on December 26, 1862, 38 Sioux were hanged simultaneously from one scaffold.

The uprising, however, was not over. It continued until the Battle of Wounded Knee in 1890, after the U.S. Cavalry had pursued the Nez Perce Indians for 1,000 miles. One famous encounter known to every North American was on June 25, 1876, on the Little Bighorn River in Montana. Here in about an hour, Lieutenant-Colonel George Armstrong Custer, his two brothers and a nephew, and over 200 cavalrymen were massacred. As noted in Chapter 10, the Sioux afterward retreated to Canada, many carrying the scalps of Custer's troops.

Because of the massive problems and bloodshed just across the U.S. border, there was great concern for the safety of the

Accompanying the force on the trek was artist-journalist Henri Julien. Since there are no known photos of the march, Julien's sketches are the only visual record. He named the one above "A Lancer of the North-West Mounted Police."

small band of red-coated policemen who headed into the Canadian West. Even Commissioner French expected "hot work" once they found the whisky; then there was the warlike Blackfoot nation that resented intrusion into its land by whites or other tribes. Against the reported 2,000 warriors the only support the *Toronto Mail* could offer the policemen was the hope that if they were scalped then

"Sharp be the blade and sure the blow,
and short the pang to undergo."

July 8 at last saw our start westward with 300 men, 310 horses, 142 work-oxen, 114 carts, 73 wagons, 33 head of beef cattle, the two nine-pound guns, and two mortars. We carried a six-months' supply of tea, sugar, flour, biscuit, and bacon; besides baggage, ammunition, and forage; also supplies of tobacco, matches, and other small articles. Much baggage was of necessity left behind, and most we never saw again. Apart from the men who had deserted and 30 horses which had died or were lost, the force generally was in good shape and spirits. We camped the first night, after a 20-mile march, on the Murray River. Thus began the real journey to which we had all been looking forward since the organization of the force. Our destination was, according to information from different sources, a strong fort called Whoop-up at the junction of the Bow and Belly Rivers, some 800 miles to the westward.

In the *Mounted Police Blue Book* for 1874, an interesting account is given in Lieutenant-Colonel French's report of the appearance of the force as it left camp for the westward march:

"On our first starting we had, of course, the usual difficulties of balky horses and unruly oxen to contend with, but after a few days we had but little trouble in this respect. Our train was, I suppose, the largest ever seen in these parts; closed to a proper interval it was a mile and a half long, but from advance to rear-guard it was more nearly from four to five miles, owing to the uneven rate of travel of horses and oxen, and the breaking of wheels and axles of that imposition of the country, the Red River cart. The column of route presented a very fine appearance. First came 'A' Division with their splendid dark bays and wagons. Then 'B' with their dark browns. Next 'C' with bright chestnuts drawing the guns and small-arms ammunition. Next 'D' with their greys, 'E' with their black horses, the rear being brought up by 'F' with their light bays. Then a motley string of ox-carts, ox-wagons, cattle for slaughter, cows, calves, mowing machines, etc., etc. To a stranger it would have appeared an astonishing cavalcade — armed men and guns looked as if fighting was to be done. What could plows, harrows, mowing machines, cows, etc., be for?

"But that little force had a double duty to perform — to

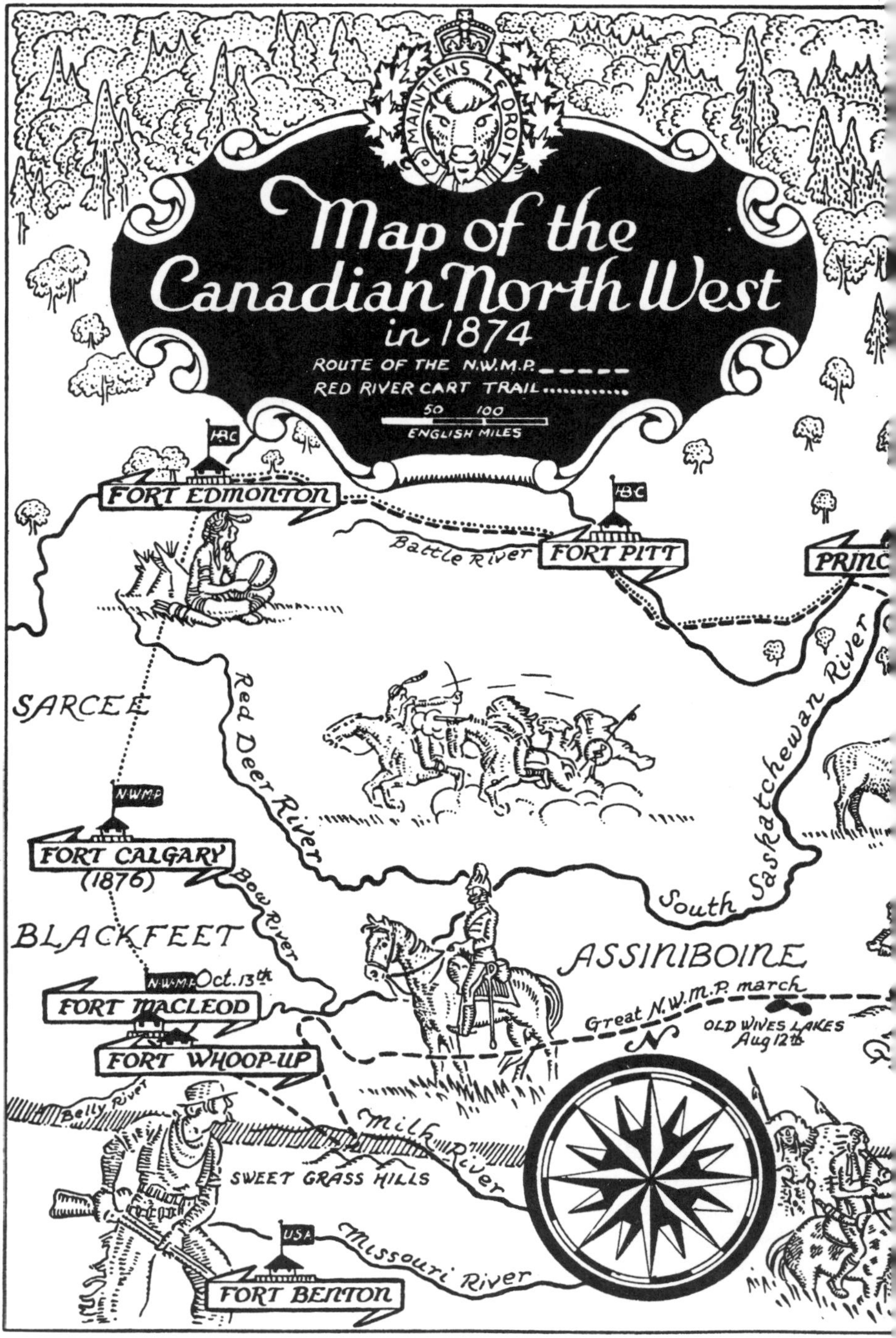

MAINTIENS LE DROIT
Map of the Canadian North West in 1874
ROUTE OF THE N.W.M.P.
RED RIVER CART TRAIL
50 100
ENGLISH MILES
HBC
FORT EDMONTON
HBC
FORT PITT
Battle River
PRINC
SARCEE
Red Deer River
South Saskatchewan River
N.W.M.P.
FORT CALGARY (1876)
Bow River
BLACKFEET
ASSINIBOINE
N.W.M.P. Oct. 13th
FORT MACLEOD
Great N.W.M.P. march
OLD WIVES LAKES Aug 12th
N
FORT WHOOP-UP
Belly River
Milk River
SWEET GRASS HILLS
USA
Missouri River
FORT BENTON

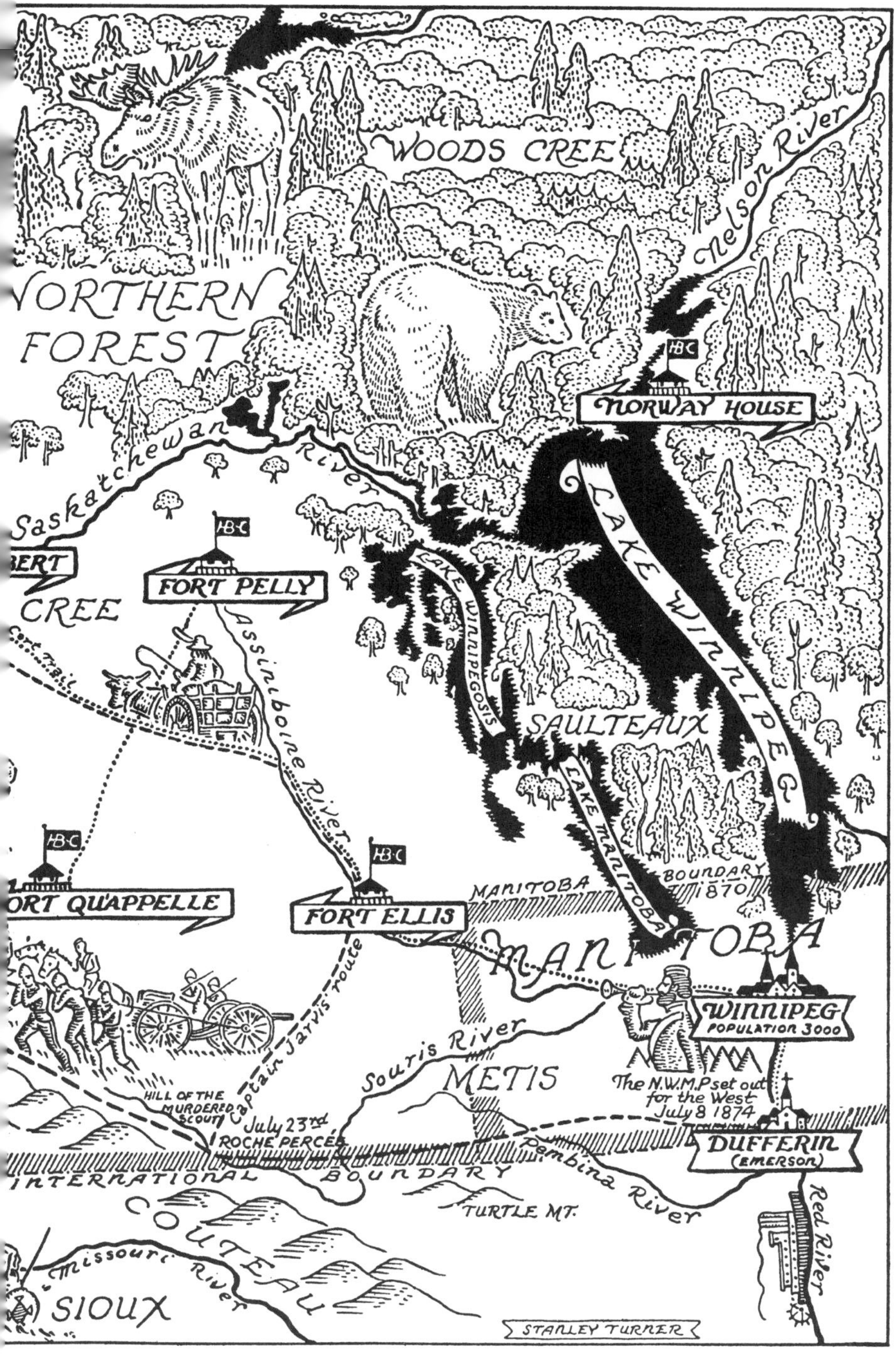

WOODS CREE
Nelson River
NORTHERN
FOREST
NORWAY HOUSE
H.B.C
Saskatchewan River
BERT
FORT PELLY
CREE
Cart Trail
Assiniboine River
LAKE WINNIPEGOSIS
LAKE WINNIPEG
SAULTEAUX
LAKE MANITOBA
FORT QU'APPELLE
FORT ELLIS
MANITOBA BOUNDARY 1870
MANITOBA
WINNIPEG
POPULATION 3000
Captain Jarvis' route
Souris River
METIS
The N.W.M.P set out for the West July 8 1874
HILL OF THE MURDERED SCOUT
July 23rd
ROCHE PERCÉE
DUFFERIN
(EMERSON)
INTERNATIONAL BOUNDARY
Pembina River
TURTLE MT.
COUTEAU
Red River
Missouri River
SIOUX
STANLEY TURNER

fight if necessary, but in any case to establish posts in the West. However, we were off at last, the only man in Winnipeg who knew anything about the portion of the country to which we were going, encouraging me with the remark: 'Well, if you have luck you may be back by Christmas, with forty per cent of your horses.' By the time the force left Dufferin the comparatively large number of thirty-one men were absent without leave, the Sioux murders of St. Joe, thirty miles west, having the effect of quickening the movements of several in this respect. I anticipated the backing out of a certain number, and fortunately brought twenty spare men, so that the force was not so short-handed as some supposed."

On July 9 we resumed our march, starting late in the afternoon. Overnight in a heavy storm 20 head of horses stampeded, but were recovered next morning. We waited half a day for the carts to catch up, the half-breeds sulking over some fancied grievance. At this camp, to save our horses, three loads of luxuries the Commissioner thought could be spared were sent back. Reports reached us of depredations committed by Sioux Indians across the Line, and for several days mounted sentries watched over the horses at night.

We travelled for a considerable way along the Boundary Survey road, which made marching comparatively easy. We remained a short time at Pembina Mountain, a beautiful spot. Here we met the first locusts, the air being literally alive with them and the ground thickly covered. Vegetation this year was devastated in Manitoba by the clouds of these insects passing toward the west. We crossed Pembina Mountain on July 13 and encountered another heavy storm that night. With hailstones the size of marbles, and lack of grass owing to the locusts, the horses fared badly and suffered in consequence. So far we had travelled at the rate of some 20 miles daily. The only game seen was a few antelope, none of which could be approached. West of Pembina Mountain we saw the first buffalo skulls, but many hundred miles had yet to be traversed before we met the living animals.

At Pembina Mountain we were joined by a party of half-breeds selected by the Governor of Manitoba. They brought presents for Indian chiefs and were supposed to assist the force as guides and interpreters. But we found later they knew nothing of the country west of the Cypress Hills, and the only Indian language they understood was Cree. Of Blackfeet, they knew nothing.

On July 17 we met a returning party of the Boundary Survey. They reported having fired on a party of Indians attempting to raid their horse herd. Our rations from this point were cut. It was evident the journey would take much longer than anticipated at the slow rate of progress, and it was doubtful if we had sufficient for the long stretch ahead.

The horses now began to give out, and the train stretched over many miles. On the 19th the rear guard under me was so far behind that we were forced to camp alone, with no water for horses or cattle or rations for the men. To make matters worse, it rained all night. We caught up with the main body at the Souris River where we rested for several days. A number of men were left at Souris River in charge of sick horses, with some transport we were unable to move. At the second crossing of the Souris we met more of the Boundary Survey returning, their work completed. Feed was very scarce, the grasshoppers being numerous, and more horses giving out, we had to leave them. The eastern horses, unaccustomed to grazing or looking out for themselves, could not stand the hardships.

On July 28 we arrived at Roche Perce. It was a full day before the stragglers came in, Colonel Macleod having remained behind to see that all arrived. The horses were in bad shape from scarcity of feed and water, hundreds of miles remained to be covered, and the prospects for a successful termination to the journey began to look none too rosy. Rations for the men were again cut, and they fared none too well. At Roche Perce, 270 miles from Dufferin, we made a long halt. A troop, in command of Inspector Jarvis, with Sub-Inspector Gagnon as subaltern, was detailed to proceed via Forts Ellice, Pitt and Carlton to Edmonton. Sam B. Steele was Sergeant-Major with this troop, which took with it 55 of the weakest horses, 24 wagons, 55 carts, 62 oxen, and 50 cows and calves. Sub-Inspector Shurtliff and 12 half-breeds also accompanied the party. Their instructions were to wait at Edmonton for further direction. They arrived on October 27 after a most difficult journey between Carlton and Edmonton, 88 days from Roche Perce. Much of the country was timbered, and it was necessary to clear miles of road for the wagons.

On Inspector Jarvis's detachment leaving for the north, we overhauled and reloaded our wagons. Most of the sick horses and men having gone with him, the main body was relieved of much encumbrance and, feed and water at Roche Perce being good, our horses picked up wonderfully. Coal found at this point was used in the forge. A week's rations were cooked in advance and wood for fuel was loaded, as it was expected no more would be found for a long distance. By July 30 our diminished force was ready for another start.

We made 26 miles on the 31st, still finding good feed and water. The weather remaining fine, the horses did fairly well and covered more ground. Up at daylight, we were on the move by 5 o'clock. Guard duty was heavy. An officer, a picket, and 15 men were detailed every night, and the officer next day had to take either the advance or rear guard. We therefore found enough to do, especially as when on rear guard we had to bring up the stragglers and exhausted teams, often arriving many hours after camp had been pitched and settled for the night. Too much praise could not be accorded the men who worked well and cheerfully under most trying and unfamiliar conditions.

The country through which we passed was full of lakes teeming with ducks and geese. We shot as many as we cared to since they made a welcome addition to the different messes. On several occasions men became lost while hunting and remained out all night, although rockets were fired to guide them into camp.

On August 3 a tornado struck the camp, and all the tents were levelled. We stood by the horses until morning to prevent a stampede. The following day I was on rear guard and, sighting some antelope in the distance, went toward them to try to get a shot. Utterly without experience of prairie peculiarities, I rode straight into what looked like a perfectly solid patch of ground. It was alkali. My horse went down until his head only appeared above the surface. I managed to scramble to firm footing as he sank, and was deeply chagrined. Marking the place, I set out for help.

I walked miles before meeting Colonel Macleod, who had a spare horse with what was called lasso harness. He had been using this horse to help teams stalled on the trail. Informed of my predicament, he returned with me. We doubted that even if we found the place we would find the horse still above ground. But after searching for a long time we located him, his head still showing above the surface. With much difficulty we got a rope around his neck and managed to haul him out. He was exhausted, and it was not until nightfall that I manoeuvred him into camp. For weeks he was unfit for work, but at length recovered. I subsequently used him on many a hard expedition.

On August 4, Colonel Macleod went south with a train of empty carts to Wood Mountain and a Boundary Survey camp. Here Colonel French thought supplies of forage and possibly pemmican might be obtained. At this point we left the Boundary Survey trail, which crossed into the United States, and thereafter we had to depend on the compass for direction. Our guides had proved most unreliable.

Colonel French states in his report of 1874: "After leaving the B.S. road, I surveyed our route as well as (under the circumstances) I could. It entailed on me a very large amount of extra work. I had to be on the alert to take the altitude of the sun and find our latitude. I plotted out the work and marked it on Palliser's map. At night I had frequently to wait up until 1 or 2

"Storm on the Third of August" Julien named this sketch. He felt that the Metis tents were far superior to the military type which he called ". . . a fraud on the prairie."

"Crossing the Dirt Hills" on September 6, 1874. By now the horses were so weak that the men had to help haul the unwieldy cannons which weighed one ton each.

a.m. to obtain the magnetic variation of the pole-star. But I was well rewarded for my trouble a month later when, without guides, I was enabled with a certain amount of confidence to strike out for the forks of the Bow and Belly rivers by compass and find the place within a short distance of that calculated on."

On the 6th we crossed a coteau (a small hill), the altitude being 3,000 ft. above sea level. We rested here a day or two. Although great prairie fires flamed to the south, they did not reach us. The pull up this coteau was a hard one on the horses, particularly with the heavy nine-pound guns. These guns gave us more trouble and crippled horses than all the rest of the transport. We had lost since leaving Dufferin 10 horses, and the carts and wagons on our line of march sometimes stretched for miles.

We had met no Indians thus far, although we were nearing the country in which they might be expected. We were also fast approaching buffalo country and were constantly on the look-out for these animals. Here the first death occurred, a man of E troop succumbing from fever brought on by wet and exposure. This event cast a gloom over the force.

On August 8 we sighted the first buffalo but could not get near enough for a kill. I was on rear guard, and can well remember the view from the top of the plateau, our party moving along in the distance, with the Old Wives' Lakes visible several miles to the west. A few buffalo grazed near the lakes. As far as the eye could reach stretched a boundless prairie, partly burned. It was indeed a wonderful sight to us who had never seen the western prairies in their wild beauty — a sight never to be forgotten by those who witnessed it.

We here sent forward for rations, as we were two days behind the party owing to our many exhausted horses. The main force was camped at the Old Wives' Lakes before we overtook it. We remained here several days, waiting for Colonel Macleod who arrived the day after we joined the camp. He brought a supply of dried buffalo meat, pemmican, and several cartloads of oats which were much needed. Horses were dying daily for want of them. Colonel Macleod again left for Wood Mountain for a further supply of forage, while we proceeded on our way westward.

Old Wives' Lakes lay some 500 miles from Dufferin. They were slightly salt, the water bad for the horses. Ducks, geese, and pelicans abounded and there was plenty of shooting.

On August 12 we met the first camp of Indians. They were Assiniboine, not an imposing lot or a good type of the plains aborigine. At this point we established what was called Cripple Camp. As grass and water were good, 14 wagons, 28 of the poorest horses, and 7 men were left, with a half-breed and some footsore cattle and stores that were not urgently needed. This party was to remain until picked up by that part of the force which would return later on. A Sergeant was placed in charge.

Our rations were cut to half a pound of bread per man a day. Sugar we had been without for some time. Colonel Macleod arrived from Wood Mountain on August 15 with a further supply of oats which did much to save the horses. On August 21 we met the first party of half-breed hunters who had been out from Winnipeg all summer hunting buffalo. Their carts were loaded with pemmican and buffalo robes. They had left Winnipeg in the early spring and had been as far west as the Cypress Hills. Their transport was ponies and carts. They reported no feed between us and the Cypress Hills, buffalo in great numbers having eaten off all the grass.

These hunting parties were annual affairs. They slaughtered thousands of buffalo, as several carcasses were required to make a sack of pemmican weighing about 150 pounds. Much of the meat was left rotting on the prairie. A hundred or more animals might be killed in a single hunt and the waste was enormous. The buffalo hunters lived a happy life, camping all summer and returning in the fall with carts groaning with their loads of pemmican and robes, the sale of which provided for the winter and enabled them to start again in the spring. Their guns were chiefly flint-lock muskets purchased from the Hudson's Bay Company, repeating and breech-loading guns being rarely seen among them.

Since they often came into collision with the Blackfeet and other Indians in the vicinity of the Cypress Hills, many were killed on both sides. They also took every opportunity to steal horses from Indian camps, the Indians in retaliation frequently setting them afoot. Then they found themselves in a bad way, but were generally rescued by other camps of half-breeds in the vicinity or the friendly Crees, who sometimes hunted near the Cypress Hills.

After leaving this party we often saw bands of buffalo in the distance but too far off to be reached. For fuel we used buffalo-chips (dried buffalo dung). It made a capital though not lasting fire. It served us during the remainder of our journey and in many subsequent trips, even in winter when we dug it from under the snow.

We found the half-breeds' report of bad water fully justified, most of it being unfit to drink, salty, or in the small ponds polluted by buffalo. On August 25 we sighted the Cypress Hills and camped near a creek of clear cold water, with good feed around it. Here we cut some hay and carried it with us. A stay of several days refreshed both men and horses. Several antelope and deer were killed in the hills, the first fresh meat we

Surveyors establishing the Canada-U.S. border near Long River about 80 miles west of Dufferin in 1872. Commissioner French wanted to follow their rough trail along the border but politicians interfered. After the first 200 miles they ordered French to head northwestward, even though none of them knew the country which offered little forage, wood or water.

Apart from the Indians, only the Metis regularly ventured onto the prairie. The sketch below by John Mix Stanley in 1853 shows Metis hunters from today's Winnipeg on their annual buffalo hunt which took all summer. In this group were 824 Red River carts, 1,200 horses and 1,300 people. Many hunters died in clashes with the Indians.

had enjoyed for a long time. The horses, however, despite the rest, were getting very poor and the work of the men was doubled through having to drive and look after so many exhausted animals. The men behaved splendidly through all the hardships, often on scanty rations.

The Cypress Hills country was well wooded, the brush loaded with berries of all kinds. In those days it was also noted for grizzly bears, but although we saw many tracks we did not encounter any of the beasts. Our line of march skirting the Cypress Hills took us not far from the site in after years of the town of Maple Creek. We little thought that only 10 years hence a great transcontinental railway — the Canadian Pacific — would traverse a country that then for hundreds of miles was without human habitation, that had pasturage for millions of buffalo, and was the hunting- and battle-ground of the wildest tribes of Indians in the North-West.

At the Cypress Hills we were nearly three months out from Dufferin and 700 miles from that point. We had yet to travel far, our stock was daily diminishing and those left daily becoming weaker. Provisions were growing short, and but for the buffalo we should have been in a bad way. We killed the first buffalo on September 1. Most of us joined in the hunt; guns popped in every direction.

I remember seeing one man riding alongside an old bull, in his excitement beating him with the butt of his empty gun until someone came to his assistance and brought down the game. We killed four, the meat making welcome addition to our bill of fare. From this point on we had no dearth of fresh meat. The farther west we travelled, the more plentiful became the buffalo. There were places where, as far as the eye could reach, untold thousands were in sight, the country black with them. They had eaten the grass short, making feed very scarce, and had also fouled the lakes. There seemed no end to the immense herds. They were easily approached, and we killed many from the saddle without going off the line of march.

From the Cypress Hills Colonel French directed the march northward toward the junction of the Bow and Belly Rivers, the point at which Colonel Robertson Ross and Palliser's map indicated the location of Fort Whoop-up. We arrived there on September 9.

The following is taken from Colonel French's report to the Government in 1874:

"We were at last at our journey's end, the Bow and Belly rivers. Three deserted log huts without roofs were the only forts visible. Here we were supposed to find luxuriant pasturage, a perfect garden of Eden, climate milder than Toronto, etc.

As far as our experience goes, that vicinity for sixty or seventy miles in every direction is little better than a desert; not a tree to be seen anywhere, ground parched and poor, and wherever there was a little swamp it had been destroyed by buffalo. A reference to my diary will show what a very serious position we were now in. We had come a distance of seven hundred and eighty-one miles from the Red River, and after the first eighteen had not seen a human habitation except a few Indian wigwams. It was now the middle of September, and the appalling fact was ever pressing on my mind that on the 20th of September last year the whole country from the Cypress Hills to the Old Wives' Lakes was covered with a foot of snow, several oxen and horses having been frozen to death. All over the country there is very little wood, and snow would hide the buffalo chips available. From what I heard of the fertility of the soil on the Bow and Belly rivers I had hoped that the horses and oxen with a few weeks' rest in the vicinity would have pulled up greatly in condition, but in reality the force had to leave there as quickly as possible to prevent their actually being starved to death. In fact several of the oxen did die of starvation, but the mistake is readily accounted for. Those who travelled along the base of the Rocky Mountains reported on the fertility of the soil on the head-waters of the Bow and Belly rivers, and somehow these reports came to be applied to the whole course of the rivers.

"On the 11th the force moved up the Belly River but could find no ford at first, the water being either too deep or too rapid. Pushing on sixteen or eighteen miles we found a ford. I sent out two reconnoitering parties from this point, one up the Belly River, and the other up the Bow River, and made arrangements to send Inspector Walsh and seventy men and fifty-seven horses through to Edmonton. The Edmonton party forded the river on the 14th; on the 13th the Belly River party returned, having travelled about thirty miles west without finding road, trail, or grass, but buffalo moving south in thousands. Inspector Denny's party did not return until late in the afternoon of the 14th. They had been up the Bow River for about eighty miles, and gave a dreadful account of the country; neither wood nor grass, country very rough and bad hills ahead. Mr. Levaillee (who was in charge of the party of half-breeds selected by His Honour the Lieutenant-Governor to accompany or precede the force with Indian presents) was with Mr. Denny and placing great reliance on his judgment I asked him if the party could get through to Edmonton. He stated it would be almost impossible to take the horses through, and that we would certainly lose most of them if we tried. With much reluctance I had to counter-order the Edmonton party, and instructed Inspector Walsh to follow the main party south to the Three Buttes."

CHAPTER THREE

Fort Whoop-up—and a Surprise

After "One of the most extraordinary marches on record...." the policemen find not "hot work" but a hot meal.

As Colonel French states in his report, I was sent up the west side of the Bow River with three half-breeds to see if any sign of a trading post existed on that river, or if I could discover any Indians or traders. We started at daybreak and killed a buffalo during the morning. On striking a small creek with some firewood we cooked the best pieces for breakfast then took a supply for future use.

During that afternoon, while riding along the bank overlooking the river, we saw two Indians on foot coming from the prairie. They were heading for a deep gully running to the stream. We tried to cut them off to interrogate them but they were too quick for us, disappearing down the ravine before we could overtake them. We rode toward the gully, but when within 300 ft. of the edge were confronted by a line of some 50 Indians, all armed, their guns pointed towards us.

With our rifles ready we kept moving in a circle and making signs to them. There seemed no danger of their being able to overtake us, as so far as we could see they had no horses. The half-breeds spoke to them in Cree, but their answers were not understood.

At length they lay down under the bank, their heads and the muzzles of their guns only showing, but they did not fire. One man stood up and went through a pantomime of signs which my half-breeds could not understand. The latter were thoroughly scared and insisted on retiring. These were Sioux Indians, they said, who would kill us if they had a chance.

The Indians seemed uncertain what to do, thinking perhaps that another party might be behind us. One waved what ap-

Artist Henri Julien titled the above and below sketches "Dead Horse Valley" and "The Sweet Grass Hills in Sight." By then the horses and oxen were dying so rapidly and the men so exhausted that Commissioner French became alarmed for the safety of the force.

peared to be a scalp. They were evidently a war party. I much wished to get near and speak with them, but on the half-breeds riding off and leaving me there was no alternative but to follow. It took all my persuasive powers to induce them to resume the journey up the river, which we eventually did, making a wide detour round the gully in which the Indians lay hidden.

We heard afterwards that this was a party of Assiniboines, afoot on the warpath. They had been 100 miles up the Bow River from the point where we met them. Here they attacked a party of white men who were camped in the valley with two or three wagon loads of goods for trade with the Blackfeet. They stole all the horses, killed one man, captured and burned the wagons, and destroyed the goods they were unable to take with them. They were later attacked in turn by a large party of Blackfeet, but got away after losing all their horses. One of the white men, Tony La Chappelle, resided for many years afterwards at Fort Macleod, opened a store there, and did well. Their indecision was no doubt lucky for us. They were doubtless at a loss to know what kind of a party we were, and my red coat must have puzzled them considerably.

After this we travelled at night, thinking the Indians might follow us, which indeed they did for at least a day as we found by their tracks on our return. We went about 40 miles farther up the river, or at least 90 miles from our starting point. There was no sign of any trail or habitation, no timber lined the Bow River, and the country was broken and hilly.

We were witnesses of a thrilling scene on this journey — thousands of buffalo swimming the Bow, at this point a considerable stream and very swift. We returned to camp on the third, travelling mostly at night in hard and long rides of at least 50 miles. The Indian ponies we rode were very tough and enduring. The last night thousands of buffalo passed us on a stampede, the ground shaking beneath their tread. We were fortunate not to be in their path.

On our arriving in camp Colonel French decided to move the whole force to the Three Buttes, or Sweet Grass Hills, in clear view 80 miles to the south. We would remain in camp there while the Commissioner and Assistant Commissioner went to Fort Benton, Montana, some 100 miles from the Sweet Grass Hills, to communicate with Ottawa and procure provisions and information. We left Belly River September 15 in a snowstorm, arriving on Milk River at the Boundary Line after a most dismal journey on the 18th, many horses giving out for want of feed. The weather continued cold, with occasional storms. We pitched the tents on the site of an old Boundary Survey camp. Here we found a few stores left by the last party,

The youngest member of the 1874 trek was Frederick A. Bagley, a 16-year-old boy bugler. He served 25 years before retiring as a Sergeant-Major, dying in 1945 at 87.

Below is Old Buck, the horse which Bagley rode during the westward journey. It lived to be over 30.

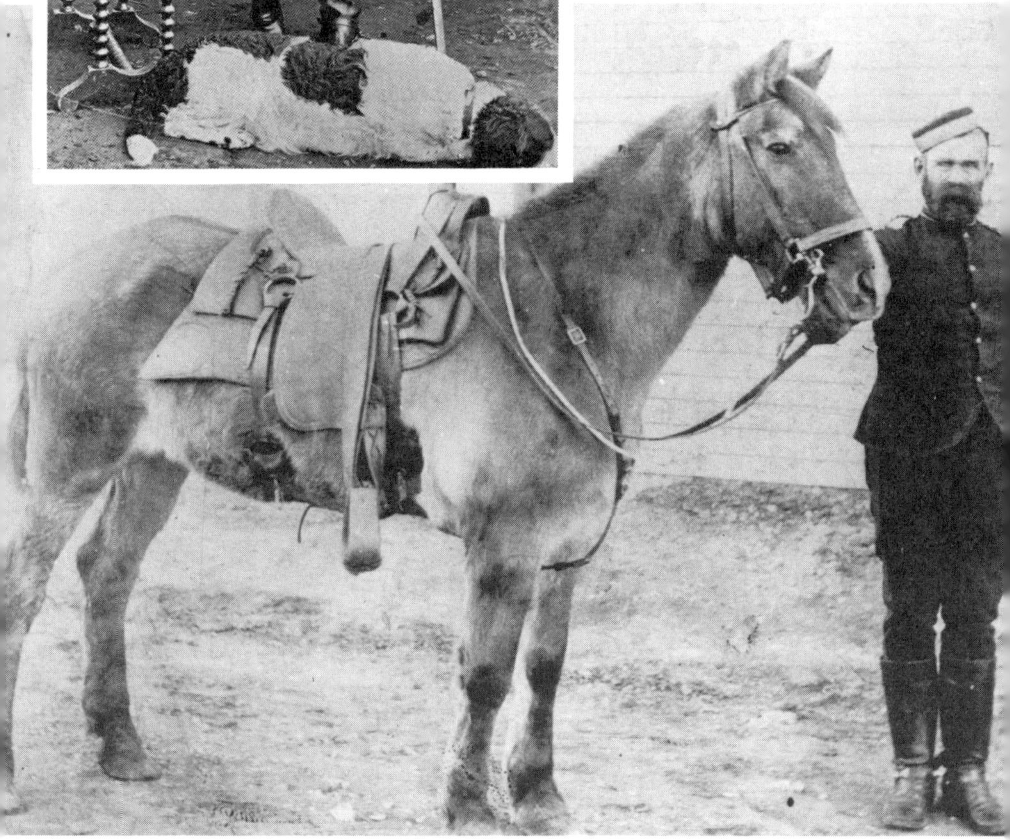

including a gallon of syrup and some sugar. These luxuries almost started a war; we had not seen anything of the sort for weeks. We also found good coal and indications of minerals.

At this point it was decided that D and E troops, with the Commissioner, would return east, gathering up en-route the stock and stores left on the way, and taking the best of the horses. We saw them off on September 21. The remaining three troops were to remain at the Sweet Grass Hills until the return of Colonel Macleod. We would then proceed westward to do the work originally planned. Colonel French and Colonel Macleod left for Fort Benton on September 22; we remained with a few crippled horses, many wagons, the two guns, and miscellaneous stores. Thousands of buffalo around us were a guarantee against starvation.

On September 29 word came from Colonel Macleod at Benton that we were only 40 miles from Fort Whoop-up. We were instructed to move camp about 15 miles west, a well-beaten trail leading to that notorious rendezvous from Benton. This trail had been continuously used for several years by the traders going back and forth. The news was most welcome. The weather had grown cold and the prospect of wintering in the vicinity of the Sweet Grass Hills was the opposite of cheerful. The messenger from Benton said the country to the west was well wooded, with many rivers and quantities of game. He also disabused our minds concerning the desperate characters of the whisky traders and Indians.

The traders were few, most of them having returned to Benton for the winter with their annual summer accumulation of robes and other furs. They also had warning of our advent; consequently, it was not to be expected we should catch many of them with whisky. The Indians, also, were amicable. They had an abundance of game and were trading with the whites without friction. Moving camp occupied two days. Our horses being few and in miserable condition, several trips were required to complete the shift. Sugar, tea, and other commodities had long since been consumed, but we had plenty of antelope and buffalo meat.

At this Sweet Grass camp the first party of traders passed with loads of buffalo robes, no doubt spoils of the whisky trade, going south. We searched their wagons but found no liquor. They were objects of great curiosity to us — the first of the far-famed whisky traders we had yet seen. The weather turned wintry and we suffered from the cold. Buffalo chips, our only fuel, gave little warmth.

Colonel Macleod arrived from Benton on October 4. He was accompanied by Charles Conrad, of the firm I. G. Baker & Company, and by Jerry Potts, a noted guide. Potts was engaged at $90 per month as a guide and interpreter.

He was a Piegan half-breed, and on good terms with all the Blackfoot tribes. A better man for his duties could not have been selected. Potts did excellent service all the years he remained with the police until his death in 1896 at Fort Macleod.

I. G. Baker & Company and T. C. Powers & Company, another equally wealthy firm, owned and operated several steamboats plying on the Missouri River between Bismarck, near the Northern Pacific Railroad and several hundred miles down the river, and Fort Benton. All supplies for Fort Benton and for the Mounted Police for years afterwards came in by this river route, then were freighted across the plains to the various police posts in what is today's Alberta-Saskatchewan.

While in Benton, the Commissioner had contracted with I. G. Baker & Company to furnish all requirements of the force for a year, and a loaded bull team was now on the way out. These bull trains were an institution peculiar to the plains. Each team of 12 or 14 yoke of oxen hauled three enormous canvas-covered wagons. There were often as many as eight teams of 24 wagons to a train. Loads ranged from 7,000 pounds up, or 10 to 12 tons to a team. Their rate of travel was slow, 10-15 miles a day, but nothing stuck them. A driver went with each team; a night herder and cook completed the outfit. Three or four horses tied to the wagons when on the move were used for night-herding the cattle. The drivers walked alongside the teams during the day, their heavy bull whips exploding as they swung them in reports like pistol shots.

On October 6, Colonel Macleod issued orders to break camp. Three troops, with Charles Conrad and Jerry Potts, moved on. The program was first an advance on and investigation of Fort Whoop-up, then a move farther west to some point to be selected for the establishment of a permanent post. I was left at the camp with my troop horse, many wagons, the nine-pound guns and loads of ammunition, for none of which transport was available. I had, besides, several sick men, a corporal, and a few others — about 20 in all. My instructions were to await the arrival of the bull teams, attach wagons and guns to the train wagons, and have accommodation made for the sick men. We were to proceed thus until we caught up with the main body.

While in camp a trader from Fort Benton — John Glenn — passed on his way to locate wherever the force determined to make headquarters. He was an enterprising man. Upon hearing of the arrival of the police, he loaded a wagon with canned goods, sugar, syrup, and a general assortment of articles they were likely to buy, and followed promptly on their tracks.

His expectations were fully realized, anything in the way

Fort Benton in 1878. Until completion of the CPR to Lethbridge in 1886, it was the main supply point for the policemen.

Jerry Potts, the scout hired at Fort Benton, was a remarkable plainsman. His sense of direction astounded the policemen, especially his ability to find his way at night and in blizzard conditions. He stayed with the force until his death in 1896 and was buried with full military honors in Fort Macleod police cemetery.

Of him, the legendary Sam Steele noted: "As a scout and guide I have never met his equal; he had none in either the North West or the States to the south."

of luxuries we had so long been without bringing the price he asked no matter how exorbitant. In this venture he laid the foundation of the modest fortune he afterwards accumulated. The men in my party, clubbing together, bought a sack of flour, a barrel of syrup, and much canned fruit. Prices were: flour, $20 per sack; syrup, $3 per gallon; other articles in proportion. These unusual luxuries were quickly disposed of; cooking went on continuously until they were gone.

The bull trains arrived a week later, our loads were attached, the sick men made as comfortable as possible and we broke camp again. The men who were well had to walk, but as the weather was cold and the daily distances covered short, this was no particular hardship. We were three days reaching the St. Mary's River where we camped not far from Fort Whoop-up. It had been searched by the troops who went ahead, but no whisky discovered. On our way to the fort we passed a dead Indian lying by the side of the road. He was an Assiniboine, killed by the Blackfeet. The body had shrivelled like a mummy's in the dry air and he was minus his scalp, which the Blackfeet had doubtless taken. We remained long enough to put the poor body underground.

Whoop-up was a stockade fort, about a hundred yards square, the dwelling-houses facing inward. The bastions at the corners were loopholed and the fort was the proud possessor of two old-fashioned brass field-guns, which I doubt could be fired without danger of bursting. Only three or four men occupied the fort, D. W. Davis, afterwards Member of Parliament in the Dominion House, being in charge. He was very hospitable, showing us over the fort, and later providing a good dinner, with fresh vegetables from his own garden. The trading room was full of goods for Indian trade. Coal, from a fine open seam near the fort, was used in the stoves.

The men in the fort all had Indian wives, acquired by purchase, probably for whisky. The women were pleasant-featured and of good physique, dressed in calico and respectable in appearance. No Indians were camped near Whoop-up. Having heard of our approach they had moved out on the plains. The traders had also been warned. If they had liquor it was hidden, which accounted for Colonel Macleod and his command finding none. We crossed the St. Mary's River a few miles above Whoop-up, following the old trail towards Old Man's River some 20 miles away.

An incident when pulling up the hill on the north side of the St. Mary's River furnished a lively interlude of fun and excitement. One of the trail wagons loaded with empty shells for the big guns upset, scattering the harmless missiles in all directions and sending the teamsters panic-stricken for cover. It was a long time before they would return. Meanwhile the team swerved, overturning a loaded wagon in which the night herder was sleeping. We expected to find him dead or gasping under the sacks of flour, sugar, and cook stoves but upon digging him out found him none the worse. The delay necessitated camp for the night.

We crossed Belly River at Slide Out, a name bestowed by the traders and retained to the present day. The Rocky Mountains, in sight since we left the Sweet Grass Hills, seemed quite near and majestic in their winter mantle. The Porcupine Hills, north of the Old Man's River, had also been visible for several days.

We arrived at the Old Man's River the fourth day from the Sweet Grass Hills. Here we found the force comfortably settled in camp on the south side near a heavy growth of woods extending for miles up and down either bank. We had a hearty welcome, glad to be at our journey's end. The location chosen looked beautiful to us after the long and weary march. And beautiful indeed it was, with the lofty barrier of snow-draped peaks to the west, the timbered range of the Porcupines to the north, and the Old Man valley as far as the eye might reach, lined with sheltering woods. Buffalo in bands dotted the prairie to the south.

Our tired horses and oxen, freed at last from the wearing drag, grazed unworried; the many tents of the force gleamed white among the trees. The scene was one of peace and loveliness, the atmosphere homelike and restful. I was glad to learn that our stay here was to be permanent. A log fort was to be built at once; indeed, the men had already started to fell cottonwood trees for logs.

No Indians had yet visited us, but the time had not been wasted as there were two prisoners in camp. They were Harry Taylor and a Spanish negro, captured the previous day by Inspector Crozier some miles up the river while endeavouring to escape south with several hundred buffalo robes and a quantity of whisky. The liquor was spilled, the robes, wagons, and teams confiscated, and the men fined $25 each, or in default sentenced to serve six months' imprisonment. Taylor paid his fine, but the negro, Bond, was unable to do so. He was confined under guard in a tent and, on completion of the fort, in the log guard-room, from which during the winter he made a bold escape. He was fired on by the sentry, but though wounded was not stopped. His body was found by Indians the following spring about 30 miles south. Taylor became a well-known citizen. After following various lines of business he settled down as a hotel keeper at Macleod.

The long march from Dufferin which lasted over four

In 1967 the Kinsmen's Club of Lethbridge built a replica of Fort Whoop-up just outside the city, complete with flag which the community adopted as its official city flag. The original Whoop-up cannon shown on page 7 is on display at the Fort.

months was ended. We were at last definitely established in the new country, the work for which the North-West Mounted Police force was created lying clearly before us. I quote the conclusion of Colonel French's report to the Canadian Government:

"I feel, sir, that in the foregoing report, I have but very inadequately represented the doings of the force. The broad fact is, however, apparent — a Canadian force hastily raised, armed, and equipped, and not under martial law, in a few months marched two thousand miles through a country for the most part as unknown as it proved bare of pasture and scanty in the supply of water. Of such a march under such adverse conditions, all true Canadians may well be proud. To the Government of the Dominion my heartfelt thanks are tendered for having placed me in a position which entitled me to claim that I was a member of a corps which performed one of the most extraordinary marches on record."

CHAPTER FOUR

Building Fort Macleod

Within the cottonwood walls of their new fort, the policemen enjoy a Merry Christmas but a tragic New Year.

Cottonwood timber suitable for building was abundant and the men were all busy felling trees and cutting them into 12-foot lengths as material for the proposed fort. Time pressed, for the season was late. Construction was rushed since horses as well as men required shelter. In trenches three feet deep, logs planted upright formed the walls, cross-logs the beams, and poles covered by a foot of earth the roofs. Clay served as plaster for the walls, inside and out. Windows and doors brought in by the bull teams were put in place and the barracks was complete. Of lumber, only enough for doors was available; the floor was bare ground.

The completed fort was a square, 200 feet to a side. Other buildings similarly constructed were run up, two long buildings on each of three sides, the stables on the fourth. The men's quarters and saddle-room on the west; stores, hospital, guard-room, and latrines on the south; and the stables, blacksmith's shop, and other saddle-rooms on the north. All buildings faced inward, their back walls the walls of the fort. A large gate at either end opened upon the square.

With everyone engaged, the fort was soon finished. Plastering in low temperatures with clay softened by water and put on with bare hands was frigid work. While the force was thus employed, I. G. Baker & Company's men were at work on similar structures for a trading post near the fort. Their store was soon finished and stocked with merchandise — canned fruit, clothing, groceries, guns, ammunition, Indian trade goods, and anything likely to find sale with the police. Prices were high. For instance, $1 a can for fruit or vegetables. As we had received no

Two Blackfoot warriors in 1874. The rifles were not for show. The tribe was continually at war with Crees to the north and with other tribes to the south in Montana. Although the names Blackfoot and Blackfeet are used interchangeably, only Blackfoot is correct.

pay since leaving Dufferin, all purchases were made on credit. Orders were taken on the men's pay, and when money at last came little was left to them after their accounts had been settled.

Patrols were sent out to look for whisky traders on their way south, trying to evade the police. There were a number of captures. The offenders were heavily fined, their liquor spilled, their robes, teams, and wagons confiscated. The Indians soon began to come in and set up large camps near us. Councils were held. They were told the reason for our coming into the country. Without exception they declared themselves well pleased at seeing an end put to the whisky trade. Hundreds of Blackfeet, Bloods, and Piegans visited us while the fort was building. They were in those days a fine lot of men, for the most part friendly. They owned hundreds of horses, lodges of tanned buffalo skins, often fancifully painted, and quantities of buffalo robes for trade. With plenty of meat in their lodges, no happier people might be found anywhere. They gave us valuable assistance in locating the whisky traders and in suppressing the traffic.

The Blackfoot nation in 1874 numbered 8,000. Of our civilization they knew nothing. They lived in summer on the plains and in winter in camp on the wooded river bottoms. Their tents, floored with buffalo robes, were warm and comfortable. Buffalo meat was their staple food. They ate little flour but were extremely fond of tea and drank great quantities. Tobacco they generally mixed with dried red willow inner bark or the leaf of a small shrub with a red berry, plentiful on the hillsides, called by them "ah-so-kin-oky." This leaf gave the tobacco a very aromatic flavour.

The women did all work in camp, setting up and striking lodges, cooking, tanning robes, sewing, etc., The men loafed, ate and smoked, or boasted of past exploits and planned raids against their enemies. They were continually at war with the Crees in the north, and with many tribes to the south in Montana. In summer or winter they would travel hundreds of miles on horse-stealing expeditions, often returning with large herds of animals. Years were required by the police to put an end to these forays, a custom of generations, and almost a part of their religion. It was meritorious to steal, and a murderer was acclaimed as a brave — a coveted distinction. The more horses stolen and the more enemies slain, the happier would be his state in the happy hunting grounds of the next world.

Prior to our arrival a few Catholic priests had at intervals visited the plains Indians, but missionary effort had been confined almost altogether to the Crees. In the north, in the shadow of the Rockies, the Reverend George McDougall had in 1871 established a small mission among the Stony Indians on the Bow River and named it Morley.

Colonel J. F. Macleod became head of the force when Commissioner French resigned over poor treatment of the men. The new fort was named after him.

Fort Macleod in 1878.

The cannon and mortars that were hauled across the prairie at Fort Macleod in 1890.

Main Street of Fort Macleod when the community was on the island.

They did good work, but it was a mistake to suppose that the character and habits of the red men could be changed in a few years and that a wild people could be made to comprehend the laws of the white man and conform to them. The Mounted Police in their dealings with these people wisely from the beginning took this factor into consideration. While the law was enforced, for several years the chiefs were often consulted as to the penalties to be imposed for offences, which among white men would have been punished by imprisonment. Thus by degrees the Indians came to understand our laws and to accept them.

In the Indian camps near the fort during this first winter there was continual dancing. At these dances, tea mixed with black tobacco, was the standard beverage. The tobacco ingredient seemed to act as a stimulant. A tragedy occurred at one of these dances, several of us being present at the time.

An old Indian, jealous of a young buck who was dancing with his young and comely squaw, left the tent. Returning, he cut a hole in the skin covering, poked his rifle through it, and shot the woman dead. She fell across the fire close to where we sat. For a time it looked as if a bloody fight would follow but the man was captured and handed over to us. Afterwards he was sent to Winnipeg for trial and sentenced to some years' imprisonment. He subsequently returned and purchased another wife.

The plains Indians in the early days were extremely jealous of their women, much more so than the Crees, and their punishments for infidelity were most cruel. Death was often the penalty, but more frequently mutilation — the nose cut off close to the face. An Indian wife was a chattel to be bought and sold for a certain number of horses. The more women could be purchased, the more buffalo robes would be tanned and traded. I have known Blackfeet with as many as 20, or even 30, women so acquired.

The Indians soon gave names to many of the police. Colonel Macleod became Stamixotokan, or Bull's Head, because this crest was on the ring he wore. Most of us were named for some part of our dress or some peculiarity. I owned a beaver coat, and thus became Kis-sta-ke-ot-sokas — Beaver Coat.

We spent our first Christmas in the new fort. At a grand dinner prepared by our chef and attended by all, buffalo hump was served in place of roast beef, but we had real plum pudding. A dance followed, our partners half-breed girls. With the exception of the McDougall family at Morley, there were no white women in the land that would become southern Alberta.

A small village had sprung up near the fort: two or three stores, a billiard-room, an ex-policeman in a barber's shop, another in a shoe store. These buildings were all log, built chiefly by old traders who settled down to legitimate business once the whisky trade was ended. In spite of all we had heard against them, we found them a very decent lot of men. They were of all nationalities, either miners, traders, or hunters. There were, of course, bad characters among them, and they were all gamblers. The harder cases did not remain long, as law and order was not to their taste.

Our guard-room was full of prisoners, one or two charged with murder. The guard-room was poorly equipped, and many men who could ill be spared were required to guard the prisoners. Since the nearest jail was at Winnipeg, an 800-mile journey across the plain, prisoners could not be sent there until spring.

That winter our time was fully occupied. Long trips and many arrests were made, and the liquor traffic in a fair way to being suppressed. Most of our horses were sent south in charge of Inspector Walsh to winter at Sun River, Montana, as it was too late to put up a supply of hay near Fort Macleod. Small quantities were purchased at $20 a ton from a trader a few miles down the river, but we depended on purchased Indian ponies for use on our various journeys this first winter. They were hardy, serviceable animals, and would find their own feed under the snow by pawing in the coldest weather.

A small police detachment was stationed some 18 miles down the Old Man's River at an abandoned liquor trading post named Fort Kipp after the original builder. It was the customary log structure, surrounded by a stockade. Inspector Brisbois was in command. Two of his men had spent Christmas on leave at Fort Macleod and left to return to Kipp two days before New Year. Little did we know that tragedy would ensue.

On that same day word was brought to the fort that a Baker Company bull team, loaded with supplies and mail for us, had arrived at Whoop-up, but would be at least a week in reaching Macleod. We naturally were most anxious to get this mail at once. No letters or papers had reached us since leaving Dufferin in June and particularly we wished to have it by New Year. I therefore asked permission of Colonel Macleod to ride to Whoop-up, pick up the letters, and return by that time.

The Colonel hesitated, but being himself anxious to hear from the Commissioner, he consented. I started on the evening, of December 31, riding a tough little Indian pony. I intended to stay overnight with the detachment at Kipp, returning to Macleod the following day. Snow on the ground made the trail faint. I had made about half the distance when a sudden change of the wind, bringing a northwest blizzard, decided me to turn back. Then the temperature fell to -20°F. I found it impossible

I. G. Baker and Company bull teams enroute to Fort Macleod from Fort Benton in 1878 and, below, waiting for the ferry to the Fort. Ruts carved by the wagons are still visible where the prairie sod hasn't been disturbed.

to make headway with the wind and snow full in my face, and had difficulty in keeping my eyelids from freezing together. The slight trail was soon blotted out. I had no alternative but to turn my back to the storm and trust to the horse to find the way to Fort Kipp.

Luckily, I was wearing a warm buffalo coat, but even this and my buffalo-skin moccasins did not prevent me suffering considerably. I only saved myself from freezing by dismounting at intervals and running beside the horse. In doing so, however, I was in danger of leading the horse away from the point for which he was making. I could see only a few yards in any direction through the blizzard.

Darkness came on, and I did not dare leave the saddle, to the pommel of which I fastened the reins, letting the horse have his head. Fortunately he had been bred in the vicinity and was wonderfully intelligent. He never went out of a walk, but kept plodding long hour after hour through the storm. Around midnight it cleared somewhat. I could see dimly ahead what I took for the steep bank of the river. I trusted to the horse and he plodded on. The storm thickened again, and for another hour nothing was visible.

Then suddenly I found myself surrounded by lighted windows. Without my realizing it the horse had walked through the open gate of Fort Kipp and stopped in the middle of the square. It was fortunate I had put my trust in his intelligence. Otherwise, we would no doubt have been lost, and I have perished.

Fort Kipp that night was a welcome haven. The comfortable rooms, with their blazing log fires and a warm meal, soon put my blood again in circulation. I inquired of Inspector Brisbois if the two men, Baxter and Wilson, who had been in Macleod had returned. His reply being that he had not seen them, we concluded they had taken shelter at a small trading post some 10 miles up the river and would come in the following day.

Next morning was clear. I rode to Whoop-up, and returned to Kipp in the afternoon with the letters. Here I learned that the horses ridden by the missing men had come into the fort, riderless, soon after I had left. A party accompanied by Indians had been sent out to search for them. Just before I started for Macleod the poor fellows were brought in, one frozen stiff. The other, Wilson, was still breathing but with arms, legs, and most of his body frozen. I took a fresh horse and rode as fast as the snow would allow to Macleod. On my reaching there Dr. Nevitt raced to Fort Kipp, only to find poor Wilson dead.

The search party had followed the trail of the unfortunate men's horses to where they had wandered in a circle, and then lain down, soon to freeze in that bitter north wind. Shortly after this sad occurrence another man named Parks, ill from the exposure and hardship of the march, died in the rude hospital at Fort Macleod. These three deaths cast a gloom over us all — our first New Year in the West. The bodies of Baxter and Wilson were brought to Fort Macleod and buried with military honours by their comrades, with whom they were great favourites.

The NWMP cemetery at Fort Macleod. The reconstructed Fort, bottom, is a popular tourist attraction in today's community of Fort Macleod.

CHAPTER FIVE

On the Trail of the Whisky Traders

In sub-zero weather without even a tent for shelter, the Mounties perform their duty — and also uncover a tale of gold and murder.

January and February of 1875 were cold and stormy months. The work the men were called upon to do was hard and new to them. On our arrival we were almost without clothing. Worse, we had no prospect of obtaining any until the following summer when supplies reached us via the Missouri River from the East. The Assistant Commissioner purchased quantities of tanned buffalo skins from the Indians, and our two tailors were kept busy day and night fashioning pants and coats of these skins. They formed the principal wear for the first police at Macleod. Our chief tailor, J. Stuttaford, worked indefatigably. If the men were clothed and spared suffering much of the credit was due to him.

Buffalo coats and moccasins were warm, but jacket and trousers of the same material were stiff and clumsy to work in. Also, traders about the fort had fired the men's minds with stories of the wealth to be made mining in Montana in comparison with which their police pay was a mere pittance. These things caused considerable dissatisfaction and grumbling, which culminated in the desertion with their arms, one night in February, of some 20 men. No doubt the traders helped them with horses to escape. They were pursued, but crossed the Line before being sighted. The American authorities, however, recovered and returned their arms.

These desertions made the duties doubly hard on the men remaining. There could be no relaxation in the task of rounding up whisky traders, and the large number of prisoners necessitated strong guards, leaving few to do the other work. We were only a handful in an almost unknown country, charged with the control of thousands of warlike Indians, of whom as yet we knew little.

The responsibility upon our commanding officer, Colonel Macleod, was heavy, and must have given him hours of great anxiety. But the firmness and justice with which the Indians were treated and the fact that what we promised we performed, combined with their recognition of the great benefits to them of the suppression of the liquor traffic, established a confidence not to be gained by force or threats. On many occasions officers, accompanied by two or three men, went into Indian camps of several hundred lodges to make arrests for crime, or put a stop to drunken orgies, without encountering opposition or resistance, although the tribes had it in their power to wipe out the whole force had they felt so inclined.

Trips to different points to gather in illegal traders continued in all weathers —journeys made in a wide territory, without trails or roads, and without assistance to our small force. Transport there was none, blankets and provisions, usually pemmican, being carried on packhorses. We camped in the open, tents being too cumbersome to carry. Because of desertions the work was made more arduous, while the scarcity of clothing was an added hardship. Little wonder if more or less dissatisfaction was at times voiced. On parade, in our uncouth garments, we were a motley crew.

About the fort, too, there was constant activity: timber to be felled, hauled out and cut up, buffalo hunted for meat, buildings to be repaired. The sod-covered roofs collapsed, the earthen floors were cold and damp. These combined miseries were enough to sap the morale of any body of men, and no praise can be too high for those who endured them during that long and trying winter of 1874 at Macleod. Also, some allowance may be made for the deserters.

A brighter side of the picture was that the Indians were most hospitable. If, in our many expeditions, we came upon them we were always made welcome. The best they had was placed before us, shelter from frequent storms given us in their lodges. Their cooking was primitive and their utensils the simplest — wooden bowls for plates, fingers for forks, buffalo horns their cups. Their meat was usually boiled, but there was always plenty of it, which they willingly shared.

Throughout the winter we also had abundant meat. Elk and deer were numerous along the river. Hunters armed with long-range rifles, lying in some gully near a herd of buffalo, killed at unbelievable distances as many as were needed. Then wagons brought in the meat. The animals covered the prairie in immense numbers. At times one might travel over miles of territory and, as far as the eye could reach, see nothing but buffalo, or ride at an easy lope through countless thousands streaming ahead and behind. It is hard to realize that in a few years the great herds were gone, but the slaughter was tremendous. Fifteen thousand robes were shipped by I. G. Baker & Company from Fort Macleod to Benton — the number traded from the Indians during the winter and spring of 1874-5 alone.

Many white hunters also brought in robes and wolf skins. Thousands, too, were killed by the Indians, not only for meat, but for their tents, which they renewed annually. A tent required 10 to 30 skins for the making. Enormous numbers died from wounds and were eaten by wolves.

The half-breeds were also a factor in the destruction, slaughtering whole herds for portions only of the meat, the remainder being left to rot on the prairie. The wolves contributed to the slaughter, as when we arrived the large grey prairie species ran in packs. They were often found near the buffalo herds, pulling down wounded animals and killing young calves. An attempt was made, when the first North-West Council was formed a few years after our arrival, to enforce a law against killing buffalo calves. But the country was so vast and the more pressing duties of the small force were so arduous that it had little effect.

Fur trading was profitable. The large grey wolf pelts brought $2 to $3, buffalo robes about the same. Beaver were numerous on the rivers and creeks, and many skins were traded. At old Fort Macleod an Indian brought in the only white beaver skin I ever saw and presented it to Colonel Macleod. He had it made into a pair of gauntlets which he wore for many years.

Towards the end of the first winter the Benton firm of T. C. Powers & Company opened a general store in Macleod. By this time there were in the village three stores: the Baker Company, with Charlie Conrad in charge; T. C. Powers, with T. Boggy as storekeeper; and Tony La Chappelle, an ex-whisky trader, who sold tobacco, candy, etc., and had also put in two billiard tables. An old Hudson's Bay Company boat builder, W. Gladstone, ran a carpenter's shop; Dan Horan, an ex-policeman, a shoemaker's shop; and Dick Kennefick, also an old trader, a blacksmith's shop. Other small stores blossomed, and one or two gambling places. These were countenanced, as there seemed no law applicable to them. Faro and poker were the games favoured, with the stakes considerable. Since these places were closely watched by the police, no serious disturbances occurred. The shooting and holdups common in such places in the western United States Territories were unknown.

From the start the gamblers held for the police a healthy respect. The two principal characters operating these concerns

One of the policemen who accompanied the author when he arrested Wetherwax was Sergeant J. Francis, seated third from the left in the photo above. He was a veteran of the Crimean War and is credited with riding in The Charge of the Light Brigade.

The sketch below by police surgeon Dr. R. B. Nevitt shows a whisky trader being tried at Spitzee Trading Post which is being used as a courtroom. At right a policeman in his winter buffalo coat acts as court orderly.

were Ace Samples and Poker Brown, both quite decent fellows with Indian wives. Samples in later years opened a ranch house and stopping place at High River, but both he and Brown eventually returned to Montana. Samples was a noted pistol shot, deriving his nickname, "Ace," from his ability at 75 yards to hit the ace of any card four times out of five. He had, it was said, killed more than one man across the border, but he never exercised his skill along this line while in our area.

A Catholic priest, Father Scollen, came to Macleod and remained the winter. He spoke both Blackfoot and Cree and was of great assistance to us. We had engaged a second guide and interpreter, Munro, thoroughly familiar with the country north. He stayed with the force for many years.

With Sergeant Francis and three men I made a three-day journey to a stream at the foot of the mountains where we had information that a trader from the south was dispensing whisky to the Indians camped nearby. The weather was bitterly cold, and the snow deep. A packhorse carried our bedding, a small tent, and a few provisions. We camped the last night with the Piegan Indians in a good lodge with many robes, some freshly killed venison, and were very comfortable.

The trader had moved up the north branch of the Old Man with his team and a quantity of robes purchased for alcohol. We confiscated and spilled a five-gallon can of this liquor in the Indians' possession. By the exercise of a little diplomacy, an Indian was secured to guide us to the trader's camp next evening. The man himself was absent, but a search uncovered 10 gallons of alcohol which we destroyed, 200 robes, and a hobbled horse.

Leaving two men at the camp, with the Sergeant, one man, and the Indian, I followed the tracks of the fugitive's mount. They led due north. It became apparent that he had warning of our approach and made a hurried departure. Why he had not destroyed the liquor we could not understand. In below-zero weather he took great chances, travelling, as far as we could see, without blankets and riding bareback. All that day we pushed on without coming up with him. We spent a miserable night without tent or covering, but, dry wood being plentiful, comforted by a rousing fire. We supped on dried meat but missed our tea. Towards morning snow began to fall. But for the Indian, who though uncommunicative seemed to know where he was heading, we would never have been able to follow the trail that day.

As night came we rode down to a heavy patch of wood on the river bottom and stumbled upon a large log house. We had not heard of anything of the kind in this vicinity, but in view of the time we had been in the country this was not strange. Several sleighs lay about and a band of hobbled horses grazed in the open not far away. Smoke rose from a stove-pipe projecting through the roof.

Leaving the Indian and the Sub-Constable on guard outside, Francis and I pushed in the door and entered. Three men and two Indian women looked up and stared. The former were drinking and playing cards. Had they not been taken by surprise, they would no doubt have offered resistance. One was Wetherwax, connected with a wholesale liquor firm in Benton. The man whose trail we had followed stated that he had known nothing of police in the vicinity, but had ridden over to this place for supplies. They were all placed under arrest. On searching the house we found a large stock of liquor and hundreds of robes and furs of various sorts.

The liquor we destroyed and, getting the horses together, loaded as many robes as they would hold on the sleighs. With the owner driving, we returned as quickly as possible to the camp we had left the day before. On arriving we loaded another sleigh, slept at the camp, and left next day for Fort Macleod, feeling well pleased with our success. It had been a hard trip. I have given these details as an illustration of the kind of work the North-West Mounted Police did during that first winter — indeed, until a much-needed respect for law and order was developed in the country.

We were three days in reaching Macleod. The prisoners were tried by the Assistant Commissioner, and fined $250 each, their robes, teams, and sleighs confiscated. Two were unable to pay their fines, the result being that they joined the other culprits in the guard-room. The third man, Wetherwax, was most defiant, threatening dire consequences to follow an appeal he would make to Washington. He failed to impress Colonel Macleod, who told him to pay his fine or go to jail. So far as an appeal to Washington was concerned, he was welcome to go the limit.

He spent a week in the guard-room. Then as hard labour was the lot of all prisoners — wood-cutting, stable-cleaning, and other jobs — he paid his fine and was released. He remained in the country, opening a small store in the cabin in which he was arrested, but later returned to Fort Benton. We saw him there in visits we paid to that town in after years, engaged in the wholesale liquor business. He bore us no grudge, and seemed glad to see us. These whisky traders, as I have said before, with few exceptions, were not a bad lot and many became law-abiding citizens.

Among the men we arrested were some strange characters. The tales they told were often of great interest. For instance, I once arrested three whisky traders not far from the Rocky Mountains. They had 50 gallons of alcohol and 600 buffalo robes, the proceeds of whisky traded to the Blood Indians.

An Indian had reported that a party of traders were camped some 40 miles up the Old Man's River and I had been detailed to take three men with our saddle horses and a pack animal and bring them in. I dropped on their camp that night and, taking them by surprise, made an easy capture. Placing a guard over the camp and building a bright fire, I concluded to remain on watch myself, letting the men, with the exception of the guard, turn in for a well-earned sleep. One of the prisoners, a half-breed Mexican, requested to sit with me by the fire. I was glad of his company, as I expected his stories would help to pass the long night. I was not disappointed.

He told me that he was born in Mexico but had been obliged to leave that country on account of a horse stealing scrape he had got into. He then for many years knocked about in most of the Western Territories, turning his hand to anything that offered. He frankly stated that he had been a horse thief, stage robber, gambler and a gold miner. During some years spent in Montana he had heard reports that to the north and across the Boundary Line, and on some of the streams near the mountains, rich gold washings were to be found. But the plains Indians, particularly the Blackfeet, were so hostile that it was impossible for a small party to venture in there and remain for any length of time without being discovered and attacked.

However, he found a partner who shared with him the cost of several horses, mining tools, and sufficient provisions to last a year. They took with them another man who professed to know the north country and the three started, skirting the mountains and prospecting as they went. Towards midsummer they came to a creek which seemed worthy of closer investigation. They followed the stream into the mountains and found a pocket where they washed out considerable coarse gold. Here they remained until late in the fall. They had accumulated about $1,000 in gold dust which was kept in two separate buckskin bags.

Then bad luck overtook them. His partner, whom he called Fellows, went one morning to look for the horses. He was followed shortly afterwards by the third man, Fred Bailey. Some hours later he thought he heard shots and started out to investigate. About a mile from the camp he came suddenly upon Bailey in the act of rifling the body of his partner, who lay on the ground. Bailey, on seeing him, fired but missed. Whereupon my prisoner shot Bailey dead.

He examined his partner, who although shot through the body, was still living. Being unable to move him, he made him as comfortable as possible and returned to camp. After catching and packing the horses he went back with the loads. Fellows had died

In addition to patrols in sub-zero cold without tents, poor food, sleeping on boards with mattresses and pillows stuffed with hay, the policemen often spent months at totally isolated posts such as Writing on Stone in southern Alberta. Established in 1889, it served for 36 years before being abandoned. Today it has been reconstructed, and is located near beautiful Writing on Stone Provincial Park.

during his absence. He covered the body with stones, but left Bailey lying where he fell and moved down the creek. He camped that night at a spot not far, he said, from where we now were. He remained at this place for several days and was visited by some Blood Indians. Although to all appearance friendly while in camp, that night they stole all his horses. He was in a bad predicament, knowing that he was in danger of being killed at any moment.

Although he saw nothing more of the Indians, he knew they were not far away. He determined to hide the bag of gold-dust he had kept. That belonging to his partner he never discovered, he said, although he looked everywhere. He placed his buckskin sack in a cleft of rock, covering it with earth and stones and marking the place by some notches on a tree nearby. Then taking his gun, a blanket and what provisions he could carry, he made his way south, travelling only by night. He was weeks before meeting a human being, but eventually he reached the camp of some cattlemen in Montana. But he had never, up to this time, had an opportunity of revisiting the spot where he had hidden his gold.

He stated that he had been induced to join the whisky-trading party solely in the hope of recovering this treasure. He made me the offer of pointing out the place where it was hidden on the condition of being allowed to escape. The story, if true, which I doubted, gave rise to the suspicion of foul play on his part.

We proceeded the following day to Fort Macleod where the prisoners were tried by Colonel Macleod and fined $200 each, the robes, horses, and wagons confiscated and the liquor destroyed. None of the men was able to pay the fine so they were sentenced to six months' imprisonment with hard labour in the barracks.

The half-breed Mexican, whose name I have forgotten, insisted before Colonel Macleod on the truth of his story. He stated that he would point out the cache if allowed to go there with an escort and with this gold pay his fine. The Colonel, like myself, was sceptical but he finally agreed and two men were sent with the Mexican to try to locate the spot. The prisoner led them to the place he had indicated and, on clearing away the earth and stones, a crevice was found in the rock. The buckskin sack had disappeared, a few remaining fragments showing that it had been destroyed by some animal. The gold it had contained was scattered and mixed with earth so that it was impossible to recover much of it or to calculate the original amount. At any rate, about $100 worth was gathered up and taken with the prisoner back to Fort Macleod. On again being brought before Colonel Macleod, the rest of the fine was remitted and the prisoner released. He returned to Montana and we never heard of him again. The remains of a human skeleton were found near the spot and the few bones buried.

CHAPTER SIX

Snow for Blankets, Buffalo for Company

Caught in a blizzard, the author and his companions spend three nights in a snow cave, with even the buffalo crowding around trying to keep warm.

In February 1875, in a second large mail from the East, Colonel Macleod was directed to proceed as soon as possible to Helena, Montana, to meet Lieutenant-Colonel A. G. Irvine. He was travelling to Corrin, about 200 miles south of Helena, and the nearest railroad point. Lieutenant-Colonel Irvine had been appointed Inspector in the Mounted Police, and on arriving in Helena was to institute proceedings to procure the extradition of the men who had committed the cold-blooded Indian massacre in the Cypress Hills. Colonel Macleod was to lend his assistance and afterward return with Colonel Irvine to Fort Macleod.

Spring was approaching, whisky trading had been largely stamped out, and the Indians were moving to the plains for their summer hunt. Colonel Macleod decided that the trip to Helena should be made in March. With Sergeant Cochrane, Sub-Constable Charles Ryan and Jerry Potts, I was detailed to accompany him.

We left Macleod on the 15th of that month, with saddle and packhorses, blankets, tea, bacon, and hard biscuits, but no tent. Behind us was a formidable undertaking, successfully launched. We had made a march that should for all time be memorable, built a fort, routed the law breakers, and won the confidence of the wild tribes of the plains. In the course of our duties we had endured much hardship, but in the right spirit and with little grumbling or complaint.

We could look back upon our work since leaving Dufferin in the previous June with satisfaction, and to the future with confidence. All, however, rejoiced that spring would soon be with us. The first and hardest winter ever experienced by the North-West Mounted Police was now almost over.

The first night out from Macleod we spent at Whoop-up with Dave Akers, the man then in charge. As we were leaving the next morning Akers pointed out two rainbow-like halos around the sun which he called sun dogs. He predicted a blizzard within 24 hours. This was the first time our attention had been drawn to this celestial portent, but we were to remember it in after years. We noted, particularly on this journey, that it nearly always was the forerunner of a storm of some kind, usually a blizzard or, if not, extremely cold weather. However, his predictions did not trouble us as we rode — depending entirely upon our guide for there was no trail — during a clear but cold day toward the Milk River, our proposed camp for the night.

We passed many buffalo herds. During the morning the Colonel took a fancy to test the speed of his horse in chasing one of the great brutes. He followed an old bull for a good mile before overhauling him, but had no idea of killing the animal. As he drew alongside the bull suddenly swung his massive head in a vicious lunge at the horse. The sharp horn caught the stirrup leather, ripping it clear away from the saddle and almost unseating him, missing his leg and the horse only by a hair. This was enough for Colonel Macleod. He dropped behind, leaving the bull to lumber on unmolested. It was not safe to trifle with those mighty beasts. One thrust of a horn might disembowel a horse, or toss both horse and rider skyward.

"Colonel, I guess you leave dem ol' buffalo bull alone after dis, hey?" said Jerry Potts.

As it was now about noon we dismounted and turned the horses out on their picket-ropes to feed, dug some buffalo-chips from under the snow for a fire and, while the Colonel's saddle was being repaired, we lunched. We had made, the guide said, about half-way to Milk River. Since the sun had disappeared in mist, it began to look as if Akers's prediction was promptly to be fulfilled. We hurried along. As night came on the storm broke, a bitter wind blowing out of the north. Before we rode down the steep banks of Milk River we were enveloped in a blinding blizzard.

The outlook was not cheerful. No wood was to be found. On the advice of our guide we unsaddled and stowed the packs under a snowbank on the north side, which gave us some protection from the piercing wind. With our hunting knives we dug a deep hole in the bank, into which we all crowded. We were in for real trouble, as the guide said these blizzards sometimes lasted for days. To attempt to return in the face of the storm would have been madness — courting death. We afterwards learned that a temperature of -65°F had been recorded during this blizzard, the worst seen in Montana in many years. That night and the following — we were stormbound for 36 hours — were, I think, the worst in the experience of any of us.

There was no grass, and had there been we would not have chanced losing our horses by turning them loose to graze. Buffalo swarmed down into the river bottom and even close to the horses, which for the day and two nights we remained were bunched together at the ends of long picket-ropes. We took two-hour shifts at holding the halter ropes and keeping the buffalo from crowding in on our animals. This seems almost incredible, but the fierceness of the blizzard and intense cold had driven all fear from the beasts, and they huddled together for warmth and shelter. Our snow-cave was damp and chilled us to the bone. We slept little, but ate at intervals, and the bacon, bolted uncooked, no doubt helped to pull us through.

The storm continued. On the second morning we decided that to remain longer meant death by freezing for both men and horses. The poor beasts had stood for a day and a half without food or covering in that terrible weather. The snow which blanketed them had been some protection, but they were in bad condition and we could only trust to Jerry Potts to guide us to Rocky Coulee, 25 miles south. Here, he told us, there would be shelter, if no wood. It was miserable work saddling and packing the horses with our numbed fingers on the morning of the 9th. A more forlorn company it would be hard to imagine as we moved off afoot through the storm. Jerry Potts led, but at a distance of only a few feet or we would have lost him in the smothering white blank. Walking brought some warmth to our stiffened frames and after a time we mounted, making better progress.

We had gone some way when we missed Ryan. I rode back, while the party waited within hail, to search for him. I found him sitting on the snow holding his horse. "What's the matter?" I asked.

"We'll never get through, Mr. Denny. You and the Colonel go on. I can't make it any farther."

I learned that he had endeavoured to mount, but was unable to do so. His buffalo-skin breeches had frozen stiff and he was unable to bend his knees. I helped place him in the saddle and we rejoined the party.

The storm persisted, but we plodded on without resting. Our guide was a marvel. He rode steadily ahead, with short stops at intervals when he seemed almost to smell out the trail, for nothing was to be seen in any direction. Toward evening the storm abated somewhat. We saw directly ahead a deep gash and rode down into Rocky Coulee, our objective, just as it became dark. Here we spent another miserable night in the open. The Colonel, Jerry, Ryan, and myself lay close together for warmth under our buffalo robes, while Sergeant Cochrane held the horses bunched under a bank not far away. I would have gone out during the night to relieve him, but the Colonel stopped me. In getting from under the robes the snow covering us would have fallen in and flooded our bed. So we lay, sleeping little, through the long and wretched night.

The sun shone brightly next morning, but it was still very cold. Cochrane and the horses were completely covered with snow, but he said he had been warm and comfortable through the night. We saddled up and, postponing breakfast, started again on foot. We hoped to reach the Marias River in a few hours. Here, we had been informed, were stationed a company of American soldiers in some log buildings. They were on the look out for illicit traders on their way across the Line into Canada with contraband arms and liquor.

We rode down the hill to the Marias in the early afternoon towards the quarters of the detachment. They saw us coming and, mistaking us for whisky traders, rode out to make a capture. Discovering their mistake, they invited us in and spared no effort making us feel at home and comfortable. We certainly were forlorn and bedraggled.

We had all suffered more or less from frost bite and our horses could barely stagger. The commanding officer, Captain Williams, was kindness itself. We did yeoman justice to an enormous meal of fresh buffalo steak and hot tea. After a comfortable night we were able to continue our journey next day to Fort Shaw. Captain Williams furnished us with fresh mounts and also sent two of his men with sleighs to carry our baggage.

Our own horses were completely used up. Three died a few days after we left the Marias. Fort Shaw was only 15 or 20 miles away, and we arrived early. Built of adobe, or sun-dried bricks, Fort Shaw was at that time the largest American post in Western Montana. General Gibbon, the commanding officer, had under him some 400 men — cavalry and infantry. He was an old Civil War veteran with a record of much service in the Indian wars. Many of his officers had with them their wives and families. The life was monotonous, their only duties having to do with depredations committed on the settlers by Indian war parties.

Montana in that day was the home of many warlike tribes — Gros Ventres, Sioux, Assiniboines, and Blackfeet — who looked upon the Long Knives (their name for United States soldiers) as their enemies. Warfare between them was continual. The soldiers never went except in force into an Indian camp, and many a poor fellow caught alone was tortured and

As the author and his companions tried to keep the buffalo from crowding into their horses for warmth, they couldn't have predicted that in just a few years the population of millions would be slaughtered almost to the last animal.

barbarously mutilated. This was the condition existing on the American side of the Line between the United States authorities and the Western Indian tribes. What a contrast to that in the North-West Territories of Canada where the Indians welcomed our residence among them. They looked upon us as their friends and deliverers from the many evils they had suffered at the hands of unprincipled white men.

After two days' rest, Colonel Macleod and party again set out for Helena, General Gibbon being kind enough to send an escort and supply the transport. I remained at Fort Shaw, the General hospitably placing a room in his house at my disposal. I was suffering from snow-blindness, a most painful affliction, and was laid up for 10 days. The General and other officers did everything possible for my relief. General Gibbon had known President Lincoln well. I have often regretted having been unable at the time to preserve in writing the many interesting stories he told me of the martyred President.

On recovering from my eye trouble and frozen foot, through the kindness of the General I was taken to Helena in a six-mule ambulance. I was sorry to say good-bye to such friends. The cordial goodwill shown us and the help rendered us at Fort Shaw will never be forgotten.

While I was recuperating at Fort Shaw the weather cleared and became warm and spring-like. The journey to Helena through beautiful Prickly Pear Canyon was most interesting. The road crossed the summit of the Rocky Mountains to reach Helena, lying in a lovely valley in the heart of the range. The capital of Montana was then a thriving mining town of some 3,000 inhabitants. Placer mining in the adjacent gulches was still the leading activity, water being brought to the workings by flumes several miles in length. Accommodation at the hotels where we put up was very good.

Our stay in Helena was made pleasant by the courtesy of leading businessmen and visiting United States Army officers who went out of their way to entertain us. The Surveyor-General of the territory, Mr. Smyth, showed us the sights, not forgetting Chinatown and the dance and gambling houses. We remained some weeks and met most of the men who had deserted from Macleod in the winter. After great hardships they had arrived in Helena, only to find their dreams of wealth easily acquired not up to expectations. The majority of them called shamefacedly on Colonel Macleod and begged to be taken back in the force. A few of the best were re-engaged.

Colonel Macleod purchased wagons, horses, and needed supplies and instructed me to take the guide and return with these to Macleod. With the men re-engaged he awaited the arrival at Helena of Colonel Irvine.

The return journey was pleasant. Spring had arrived and the only difficulties we met were in fording the rivers where high water and running ice made the crossings dangerous. We found the guard-room at Macleod full, many more arrests among the whisky traders and Indians having been made in our absence. Much work also had been done. The men's quarters and the stables had been enlarged and better roofs provided. Considerable lumber had been whipsawed by half-breeds who had come down from the north and settled near the fort.

Colonel Macleod arrived shortly after us, but remained only a week before returning to Helena. Colonel Irvine had changed his route. Instead of coming via the Utah Northern to Corrin, he would travel by steamer up the Missouri to Benton, and the first boat would not arrive until early in June. It was August before Colonel Macleod and Colonel Irvine actually arrived. Colonel Irvine at once proceeded overland with escort and transport to Winnipeg, taking with him all prisoners who had been sentenced to lengthy terms.

CHAPTER SEVEN

Building Fort Walsh and Fort Calgary

One is today a National Park; the other, Canada's well known "Stampede City."

Soon after the spring break-up, Inspector Walsh came in from the Sun River camp with the horses in good condition and was instructed to take his troop, B, to the Cypress Hills and construct a fort similar to that at Macleod. The site selected lay in the center of the hills, 200 miles to the east, not far north of the American boundary. This region was infested by whisky traders. It was a favourite hunting ground for many Indian tribes who were continually coming into conflict, with horse stealing rife. Briefly, it was about as lawless a section as could be found in the Territories. It was to put an end to this state of affairs that Fort Walsh was established in the summer of 1875. Major Walsh and his troop soon stamped out the whisky trade and did much to gain the goodwill of the various Indian tribes that were accustomed to visiting the fort.

A small village sprang up, with the firm of T. C. Powers & Company opening a general store. All supplies came in by way of Benton and bull teams. In the north Inspector Jarvis and A troop passed a busy winter at Edmonton, living in the old Hudson's Bay fort, then in charge of Chief Factor Richard Hardisty. They made numerous hard trips in pursuance of their duties, and gained much useful information. A troop under Inspector Jarvis also built the fourth North-West Mounted Police establishment on the present site of Fort Saskatchewan, 20 miles down the Saskatchewan River from Fort Edmonton.

July 1875 was a month to become memorable in Canadian North-West history. On a day in that month the Hudson's Bay Company steamer *Northcote* arrived at Fort Edmonton on her maiden trip, the first boat to navigate the Saskatchewan. She

Blood Indians in front of Fort Calgary in 1878. The author, who chose the name, is seated in the chair, right center. A Gaelic word, Calgary means "clear, running water."

On July 18, 1875, the sternwheel steamer *Northcote* became the first vessel to ply the Saskatchewan River. She also brought the policemen their first mail in over a year.

brought for A troop the first mail of any consequence since camp was struck at Dufferin more than a year before.

In the spring of 1875 orders were issued that one troop from Macleod should proceed north to the Red Deer River, about 200 miles, and there await the arrival of General Selby Smyth, the imperial officer in command of Canada's Militia forces, and an escort from A troop at Fort Edmonton. General Smyth was the first man to make a tour of the North-West Territories under police escort. Inspector Brisbois was in command of F troop, while I was the other officer. The troop was full strength and had 100 good horses, with wagons for all supplies, tents, forage, and troop baggage. The program was that after meeting the General at the Red Deer and escorting him to the Bow River, a site was to be selected on that stream and a fort built for permanent occupancy by this troop.

The Bow River was hunting and winter camping headquarters of the Blackfeet and the Sarcees. Occasionally the Crees in large camps from the north met there whisky traders from the south who slipped into the country without our being aware of it at Fort Macleod. With a frontier extending for hundreds of miles they could choose their own point at which to cross into the Territories, dispose of their liquor and be back over the Line again before men could be sent to Bow River.

We did not start on the Red Deer trip until August 18, 1875, shortly after the return of Colonel Macleod with Colonel Irvine from Helena. The attempt to extradite the men wanted for trial in connection with the Cypress Hills massacre failed. It could not be proven that it had occurred on the Canadian side of the Line.

Upon the resignation, a few months later of Colonel French who returned to England, Colonel Macleod was appointed Commissioner of the Force.

When F troop left Fort Macleod, Inspector Winder remained in command with one troop of 50 men and a busy time ahead in improving the fort and in patrols. With government contracts for supplies at very high figures, the American firms in business in Macleod became wealthy in a few years. It seemed a pity that this money, amounting to millions, should go out of Canada, as it did for nearly a decade.

Previous to our leaving Macleod the first cattle — a few cows — were brought into that district by Joe McFarland who located a ranch some three miles below the fort on the Old Man's River.

We crossed the Bow River about half-way between Blackfoot Crossing and the site of the present city of Calgary, having as guide J. Munro. There were no trails. The Bow was very high and about 200 yards wide. We swam the horses and improvised a boat by tying together a couple of wagon boxes, wrapped around with wagon covers coated with axle grease. In this contraption we ferried everything over. The boat was buoyant and carried a good load, but even so the crossing occupied two days. As the weather was warm, the hours spent in cold water did not bother us.

Some 40 miles north of the Bow River the prairie ended and the wooded country began. The travelling was heavy without roads, and with many swamps and small creeks to cross. Ducks and geese were plentiful and we lived mainly on them. The mosquitoes were frightful, driving the horses wild and almost ungovernable. Smudges were kept burning all night to give the worried brutes the protection of the smoke. They needed watching to prevent their standing in the fire and injuring their hoofs. To our relief, as we neared the Red Deer the pests became less numerous.

We were six days from the Bow to the Red Deer River, and we went into camp on the south side. A half-breed occupied a cabin on the north side, and as he had a boat we made visits to his camp. We had a regular course of mounted drill in this Red Deer camp in anticipation of an inspection on meeting General Smyth. We noticed trees along this river scarred as much as 30 feet up in the spring floods by ice jams, the river in some years overflowing its banks and covering the valley with many feet of water.

Word came that General Smyth, with the police escort, would cross the Red Deer at a ford 40 miles above our location, so we struck camp and moved up the river to that point. The travelling through swamp and thick brush, plagued by flies and mosquitoes, was terrible and we were with difficulty able to control the horses. We arrived just a day ahead of General Smyth's party, which also had a very hard journey. Their horses were in a bad way from hoof disease caused by almost constant travelling through mud and water. It was necessary to leave many behind.

General Smyth inspected our troop at the camp and complimented us on our appearance. He then proceeded south with escort. Accompanied by Colonel Macleod , he crossed the Bow River at the same place and in the same manner as we had, visited Fort Macleod, and from there returned east via Benton and the Missouri River.

F troop then moved south to a point already selected at the junction of the Bow and Elbow Rivers. A bull train with supplies and extra men had already left Fort Macleod to meet us here. In addition, I. B. Baker & Company had contracted to cut and raft timber down the Elbow River for a fort to be built at a point to be selected by us near where that stream entered the Bow.

We crossed the Bow River a little above the mouth of the Elbow, finding a good ford at this place. The view from the hill on the north side of the Bow, when we reached it at the begin-

The fearless Superintendent James M. Walsh after whom the post was named.

Among men stationed at Fort Walsh in 1878 was Constable James H. Schofield, opposite page. In the background is an Assiniboine tipi.

Below: Fort Walsh in the Cypress Hills in the 1880s. It became a very important post during the problems with the American Sioux Indians.

ning of September 1875, amazed us. Before us lay a lovely valley, flanked on the south by rolling hills. Thick woods bordered the banks of both streams; to the west towered mountains with their snowy peaks; beyond the Elbow stretched another wide valley, with heavy timber farther west along the Bow. Buffalo in large bands grazed in the valleys, but of man we saw no sign. Indeed, toward the south no human dwelling existed nearer than Fort Macleod , though at Morley to the west the Reverend George McDougall had established a small mission among the Stony Indians.

In fact, except for roving bands of Indians, all this vast country for 1,000 miles to the east at Winnipeg and 200 miles to Edmonton in the north was utterly uninhabited. Our first sight of this enchanting spot was one never to be forgotten, one to which only a poet could do justice. It was by far the most beautiful we had seen since our arrival in the West. After our trying journey we felt that we were amply repaid for all we had undergone. The knowledge that a fort was to be built here, and that it would become our permanent residence gave us all the greatest satisfaction.

A small tent near the mouth of the Elbow River, a white speck in the distance, at length attracted our attention. We wondered what solitary individual could be sheltered there. We found afterwards that it was occupied by Father Doucet, a Catholic priest not long out from France. He had been sent from the mission at St. Albert south to the Bow River to study the Blackfoot speech, it being the intention to open a mission at Fort Macleod to which he would be appointed. His only companion was an Indian boy and he was delighted to see us.

We pitched camp near the mouth of the Elbow. As it would be some time before the fort was built, we placed the tents in excavations dug two or three feet deep. Some of the men, desiring more substantial shelter, built small huts. By a bull train which arrived a week or so after us we received our winter clothing and a number of small sheet-iron stoves. Since fuel was abundant we were soon very comfortable. There was plenty to be done. Besides a fort to build, dry firewood for winter had to be cut, floated down to the boom we stretched across the Elbow River, hauled out on the bank and stacked.

Some of I. G. Baker's men who had arrived with the bull train cut hundreds of spruce and pine logs for the fort and drove them down to this boom. We chose a site for the fort on a plateau of high ground at the forks of the two rivers. In trenches three feet deep we set upright 12-foot pine logs side by side to form the stockade and the outer walls of the buildings, which faced inward. The men's quarters were on one side of the square; store-room and shops opposite; on the north, stables for 50 horses; and on the south, officers' quarters and guard-room. The pole roofs were covered with earth and the log walls mudded with clay. The whole formed a square of 150 to 200 feet, with a gate at either end. At first, having no lumber, the floors were bare earth which when continually moistened became as hard as brick. Large stone fireplaces were built in all the rooms. This work was done by John Glenn who had taken up a ranch at Fish Creek, a little to the south, the preceding fall. He had put up considerable hay and this we purchased, securing a sufficient supply to feed the horses for the winter.

No Indians visited us until we had been a month in camp, but quite a number of half-breeds from Edmonton arrived with their Red River carts and built cabins on both sides of the Elbow. Before winter a little settlement had sprung up. The half-breeds did considerable freighting for us to Fort Macleod, then in the following year took a quantity of flour and other supplies from the fort to Inspector Jarvis's troop at Fort Saskatchewan. The average load was 500 pounds per cart.

I. G. Baker's men also erected a building on the flat for a general store and several log houses for residences. The enterprising ex-whisky trader, Harry Taylor, brought a billiard table all the way from Fort Benton and built a hall which was also used for dances. He sold home-made beer, candies, etc. From Morley the Reverend George McDougall visited us and erected a small church. It was the first place of worship in Calgary, a little west of the fort, in which he held services upon alternate Sundays.

In the previous year a small Hudson's Bay Company Store had been built on Ghost River, not far from Morley. This building they tore down and rebuilt on the east side of the Elbow. They had an assortment of goods which included flintlock muskets, Hudson's Bay hooded duffle capots, pigtail tobacco sold by the fathom, carrot tobacco in three-pound rolls, the heavy Hudson's Bay knife which could be used as a hatchet when required, and many other articles which had been traded by this company for generations.

After the two stores were built the Indians began to come in with large quantities of pemmican and some fall robes. Buffalo robes are prime only during the winter, and these came in later. Both stores did a good business. In the spring, 15,000 buffalo robes were shipped south by bull teams through the firm of I. G. Baker & Company alone. How many went from the Hudson's Bay Company north I do not know, but certainly a large number.

David McDougall of Morley also took considerable fur, traded from the Stony Indians, to Winnipeg in the spring. He journeyed across the plains with carts, returning with goods for another

Above: Fort Walsh in 1965, the civilian graveyard in the foreground.

Below: Today, the Fort has been rebuilt and is the centerpiece of Fort Walsh National Historic Park.

Opposite: This sculpture depicts the cooperation between the NWMP and the Indians. As Chief Crowfoot noted: "The Mounted Police have protected us as the feathers of the bird protect it from the frosts of winter."

year's trade. D. W. Davis, whom we first met in charge of Fort Whoop-up on arriving in the country, was now with I. G. Baker & Company in charge of their men building the fort. He later assumed management of the store built for that firm with a large stock of general merchandise. Sergeant Kinghorn, who took his discharge after our arrival at Bow River, engaged with this firm.

Our fort was finished at Christmas. We were glad to move into it, as our camp outside was getting decidedly cold. We found the remains of an Indian and also those of a white man lying near the Elbow River. They had been killed in a drunken fight the previous year. Many such relics had been seen by us since our arrival, mute evidence of the lawlessness that had prevailed previous to our advent. Now all was changed. The Indians of different tribes could camp near each other in safety; the liquor smugglers had given up their sinister trade, only a few of the more daring now and then trying to evade the police. Selling whisky to Indians had become too risky a business, those who still took chances dealt only with the whites and half-breeds.

I rode down to Fort Macleod a week before Christmas, leaving all well at Bow River. The fort had not been officially named, although Inspector Brisbois, without the Commissioner's authority, had named it Fort Brisbois in all his official correspondence.

Things had been going well at Macleod, and better roofs had been put on the buildings. Colonel Macleod had brought up Mrs. Macleod and Inspector Winder and Sub-Inspector Shurtliff had also been joined by their wives, so that there were now three ladies in the barracks. Sub-Constable Gallagher had left the force and started to farm nearby. His wife had also come up. These ladies all came by way of the Missouri River to Fort Benton and then made the long journey across the plains to Macleod. It was quite an undertaking for women unused to the hardships of the West, and proof of great courage on their part.

An old trader named Fred Wachter, but nicknamed Dutch Fred, had begun farming on Belly River. He made a small fortune out of the vegetables which he sold to the police for several years. He shot and killed his partner a year later and was tried for murder. But as there were no witnesses he pleaded self-defence and was acquitted. Joe McFarland and Henry Olsen brought in the first cattle, a few cows, located a few miles down the Old Man's River, and did very well in after years.

Since Inspector Jarvis's troop at Edmonton had received no pay for a long period, the Commissioner instructed me to return to Bow River and proceed as soon after Christmas as possible to Fort Saskatchewan with the money. I returned to Bow River on Christmas night and found a Christmas dinner in full swing. It was given by the non-commissioned officers, with all civilians of the village invited. Everyone had a good time, a dance following in the Taylor billiard hall. The ladies, who attended in numbers, were the half-breed belles, well dressed and some very good looking. Many of these old-time dances held at Macleod and other posts were far ahead, in the way of fun and hearty exercise, of the prim and select affairs usual after the country became settled.

In 1875 the first domestic cattle came into the country south of the Saskatchewan River. Thomas Lee, who gave his name to Lee's Creek, was the pioneer cattleman in the Pincher Creek district. In the same year a man named Armstrong with his family and another named Morgan arrived from Montana and located on the Old Man's River above Fort Macleod. This was known as Mrs. Armstrong's ranch. She did a profitable dairy business, receiving as high as 75 cents per pound from the police for butter. Also in 1875 a man named Shaw drove a herd of cattle through the Rockies by the Kootenay Pass and wintered near Morley. His stock was principally beef steers, which were readily disposed of at the police post on Bow River.

The Commissioner in 1875 established a farm at Pincher Creek, Sub-Inspector Shurtliff being placed in charge. All the mares brought in from the East were sent here and a stallion purchased, the idea being to breed horses for the force. Grain was also grown. The farm did not prove a success, however, and was sold after a few years, with a band of young breeding cattle purchased for the Blackfeet which they had refused to take after the treaty of 1877. So long as the buffalo remained on the plains, Indians would not eat beef. It was "bad medicine" they said. Pincher Creek was the name given this place by the police detachment sent there in 1875 because they unearthed an old pair of rusty steel nippers. The name stuck.

While the buffalo roamed the plains it was useless to let range cattle run. The bulls would attack and kill the domestic steers, and the cows were carried away in the great migratory herds. Therefore, such cattle as were brought in during the first five or six years of the police regime were generally herded along the river bottoms.

Shortly after Christmas I left for Fort Saskatchewan, taking with me the guide Munro and Constable Johnstone, and the pay for Inspector Jarvis's troop. I expected to return with a prisoner. We used single-horse flat-sleds, and with plenty of buffalo robes they were comfortable to ride in. We carried oats for the horses and the necessary camp utensils, but no tent. Since the country was wooded we could build brush shelters. The trip occupied six days owing to the deep snow after passing the

Red Deer River. We had below-zero temperatures but, well-clothed and running much of the time, we did not mind it.

In the absence of a road to Edmonton, we had to depend altogether on our guide. The territory north of the Red Deer abounded in big game and we saw many deer, moose, and caribou. We saw no buffalo, although a few bands were reported by Indians to be ranging along the Peace River. We remained overnight at Fort Edmonton, enjoying the hospitality of Chief Factor Richard Hardisty, the Hudson's Bay Company officer in charge.

The fort was heavily stockaded, with bastions at the corners, and was built of squared pine logs. It comprised a number of buildings, including stores, warehouses, the Chief Factor's residence, and the officers' quarters. It was well stocked with trade goods. A few half-breeds lived in cabins and some Cree Indians in lodges near the fort. Heavy timber covered the whole country beyond. A number of visitors with dog trains had recently arrived. The howling of the dogs inside the stockade at night made sleep impossible for us but did not seem to

The interior of Fort Edmonton in the 1870s.

trouble the company's people who, no doubt, were accustomed to it from childhood.

The Chief Factor expressed himself as much gratified over the change in the country since our arrival. The truce between the different Indian tribes enabled them to carry on their vocation of hunting without fear of attack. He gave us due credit for this, as well as for ending the lawlessness that had prevailed prior to our advent.

He pointed out to me logs of the fort both inside and out pitted by bullet-marks made at times when bands of Indians engaged in drunken warfare. A small brass field-gun of ancient pattern in each bastion commanded the outside walls. In the front gate was a small log-shuttered window through which goods had been passed in exchange for furs when some southern tribe, such as the Blackfeet, came to trade. On these occasions, should any Crees be camped near they were likely to take shelter in the fort until the departure of their hereditary enemies, who were eager for their scalps. Peace and contentment had now supplanted all this.

Piles of dried and frozen fish for dog feed were also stored in the fort, and quantities of dried buffalo meat taken in trade during the summer. Numerous large flat-bottomed boats, called "bateaux" by the half-breeds, were under construction. They would be used to transport furs, pemmican, etc., to Hudson Bay in the spring. These scows were of several tons' capacity. By way of the Saskatchewan they journeyed from Edmonton to Lake Winnipeg, then via the Nelson River to the Bay. They returned to Edmonton from York Factory with fresh stocks of supplies and trade goods just before winter set in, the round trip occupying from the break-up of the river in the spring to its closing again in the fall.

Hardy crews of Indians or half-breeds manned what was called a brigade, numbering 20 or more boats. Portages were frequent, and on the return journey against the stream the boats were towed for hundreds of miles by gangs of men with "tracking" lines, working in relays of a few hours each.

These voyageurs were a stalwart type, peculiar to the service of the Hudson's Bay Company, certain families having followed the calling for generations. They were inured to water, in which most of their summer working hours were spent. They were satisfied with gaudy scarfs and blankets, tobacco, and a little flour and sugar, or other goods occasionally, as pay for their work. Game and fish were plentiful everywhere en route, so that they had always an abundance of good sustaining food. The winters they spent about the different Hudson's Bay Company posts in dancing, feasting and drinking when they could procure liquor. Occasionally they went south to hunt buffalo.

CHAPTER EIGHT

Join Us on the Warpath

"Together, we can easily destroy all of the police posts," was the Sioux's invitation to the Blackfoot.

At Fort Saskatchewan we remained several days. The fort had been built that summer and was patterned after Macleod and other forts. The troop had comfortable quarters, having been able to procure shingles for roofing the buildings, thus escaping the discomfort we experienced at Macleod and Bow River where the earthen roofs leaked badly, both during and after rain. Troop A had passed a quiet winter. They had not been required to make the long hard journeys after smugglers as had troops in the south and, since the country was wooded, they had always good fires to brighten their camps when on patrols. No whisky traders had come so far north; their work was therefore chiefly the apprehension of those guilty of petty crimes among the Crees and half-breeds.

They had several prisoners in their guard-room, one of them, George Godin, or Kis-ka-was-is (his Cree name), who some years previously had killed his wife in a most atrocious manner, and most brazenly defied such authorities as were in the country before the arrival of the police. He had been held in jail by Inspector Jarvis pending an opportunity to send him south for trial at Fort Macleod. I took him with me on my return to Bow River. He was a sullen brute. I took no chances with him, handcuffing him at night to Constable Johnstone and putting him in leg irons during the day to forestall any attempted break for liberty. The journey south took the usual six days' heavy travelling, the snow being very deep.

We found the Commissioner, Colonel Macleod, and Colonel Irvine who had been appointed Assistant Commissioner, awaiting us at Bow River. They had two dog trains, and were on the way to visit Fort Saskatchewan, but required the guide Munro

In the event of war, the most vulnerable of the police posts was Fort Pitt which didn't even have drinking water. It is shown above shortly before the Riel Rebellion. At left center is Big Bear, and sitting on the Red River cart is Corporal R. Sleigh who was killed in the fighting

In charge of the Fort was Inspector Dickens, right foreground with beard and sword. During the Rebellion it was captured by Big Bear and 200 Crees, Dickens and his men retreating to Fort Battleford.

to accompany them. On my arrival the question of a name for the Bow River fort came up. After many had been discussed, Colonel Macleod mentioned an old castle in the Isle of Mull that once belonged to the Macleod clan. It was called Calgary, which he stated meant in Gallic, "Clear Running Water." This so appropriately fitted the waters of the Bow and Elbow Rivers that it was immediately adopted by us all. That night it came out in orders that in future the fort should be known as Fort Calgary, subject to the approval of the Minister of Justice. This approval was afterwards given, and the name of Calgary came into being.

It was never spelled with two "r's" as often stated. Stories without number have been written as to how the place was named, not one being correct. I therefore have given a detailed account of its christening, having been one of three who decided on the name in February 1876.

The half-breed murderer, Kis-ka-was-is, was tried, sentenced to hang, and sent to Stony Mountain Penitentiary. He was, however, reprieved owing to the intercession of the Catholic Church and afterwards returned to Edmonton. He was later re-arrested for horse-stealing, escaped, and still later was arrested in Montana for murder there. Sentenced for the second time to hang, he again escaped, turned up on the reserve west of Edmonton, was recaptured, and returned to Montana. He eventually died in jail, ridding the country of about the worst character it was ever my lot to come across.

Inspector Brisbois resigned from the force this spring, and I remained in command of F troop at Fort Calgary during the summer of 1876. Mail was now carried monthly between Fort Benton, Macleod and Fort Walsh, and travel between these last posts was frequent. Walsh was a very important post, owing to the number of United States Indians who hunted near there on what was jealously regarded by the Canadian tribes as their special preserve. The Sioux and Assiniboines, the principal offenders, had always been deadly enemies of the Blackfeet. This situation was the cause of much anxiety to the police.

The fact that thousands of Sioux and Cheyennes were at war with American troops in the Blackhills country south of the Missouri River, not far from the Canadian boundary, added greatly to their worries. Our force was so small and the duties so arduous that we had little rest from patrols to Indian camps, often several hundred miles away. Summer or winter, there were innumerable journeys to Fort Walsh, to Edmonton, and to other parts where trouble was reported. We had become accustomed to the work by this time. I doubt if a hardier or more courageous body of men ever existed than that first small force of Mounted Police who patrolled the plains in the early 1870s and 1880s.

In 1876 control of the North-West Mounted Police was transferred from the Department of Justice to that of the Secretary of State, and Lieutenant-Colonel Macleod succeeded Lieutenant-Colonel French as Commissioner of Police. Two troops were moved from Fort Pelly to strengthen the force at Fort Walsh and Fort Macleod. The massing of the force at these posts near the frontier no doubt secured tranquillity in that section of the territory and prevented the American Indians from using Canadian soil as a base of operations for prosecuting the war with the United States troops.

The following extract is taken from my report in 1876 to the Assistant Commissioner which was forwarded to the Honorable R. W. Scott, Secretary of State:

"According to orders received on 8th July, to proceed to the Blackfoot camp for the prisoner Nataya, I left Bow River on the above-mentioned date, and found the Blackfeet camped about thirty miles above the mouth of the Red Deer River, being about two hundred miles north-east of Elbow River.

"After having secured the prisoner I was detained in camp by a council called by the principal Blackfoot chiefs, who invited me to their meeting. They told me they were very glad I had arrived, as at that time they were in a very unsettled state owing to communications that had passed between the Blackfoot nation, including the Blood and Piegan Indians, and the Sioux from across the Line. About a month ago the Sioux had sent a message to the Blackfoot camp, with a piece of tobacco, which the Blackfoot chief showed us. The message told the Blackfeet from the Sioux that the tobacco was sent them to smoke if they were willing to cross the Line and join the Sioux in fighting the Cree Indians and other tribes with whom they were at war, and also the Americans whom they were fighting at the same time. The Sioux promised to give the Blackfeet, if they would join them, plenty of horses and mules they had captured from the Americans.

"They also told the Blackfeet that they had a number of white women whom they had taken prisoners. These they also promised to the Blackfeet if they would join them. They also told the Blackfeet that if they would come and help them against the Americans, after they had killed all the whites, they would come over and help the Blackfeet to exterminate the whites on this side. They also told them that they knew that the soldiers on this side were weak, and it would take but a short time to capture any forts they had built here, as they had taken many strong stone forts from the Americans with small loss to themselves. The Blackfeet had sent an answer to the Sioux a short time before I arrived to the effect that they could not smoke their tobacco on such terms, and that they were not willing to make peace with the understanding of helping them to fight the whites, as they were friends and they would not fight against them. The messenger from the Blackfeet to the Sioux had just returned when I arrived at their camp, with the answer the Sioux had sent.

"They said that as they would not come and help them against the Americans, they would come over to this side and show the Blackfeet that white soldiers were as nothing before them, and that after they had exterminated the soldiers and taken their forts, they would come against the Blackfeet.

"In consequence of this message the Blackfeet nation, when I reached their camp, were in a state of uncertainty, not knowing how to act. Crowfoot, the head chief, was authorized by the nation, many of whom were present, to ask me whether in case they were attacked by the Sioux, without themselves being the aggressors, and they called upon us, the Mounted Police, to help them, would we do so? I told them that if the Sioux crossed the Line and attacked the Blackfeet without cause we were bound to help them, they being subjects of the country, and having the right to the same protection as any other subjects.

"Chief Crowfoot told me in these words: 'We all see that the day is coming when the buffalo will all be killed and we shall have nothing more to live on, and then you will come into our camps and see the poor Blackfeet starving. I know that the heart of the white soldier will be sorry for us, and they will tell the Great Mother, who will not let her children starve. We are getting shut in. The Crees are coming into our country from the north and the white men from the south and east. They are all destroying our means of living, but still, although we plainly see those days coming, we will not join the Sioux against the whites, but will depend upon you to help us.'

"The chief then told me that the Blackfeet had told him to tell me that as we were willing to help them, they would in case of being attacked, send two thousand warriors against the Sioux.

"I thanked them for this offer, and told them I would inform you of all they had told me, and that as long as they were quiet and peaceable they would always find us their friends and willing to do anything for their good. They expressed great satisfaction with all I had told them, and promised to do nothing without letting us know and asking our advice.

"I distributed some tobacco among them, and told them to let us know of any movement of the Sioux to the north. I left them on Friday last, camped all together about thirty miles above the mouth of the Red Deer. I brought the prisoner with me without any trouble and arrived here this day."

A copy of the report eventually reached Queen Victoria. The following reply was received from the Governor-General:

"Her Majesty has commanded me to instruct you to inform the chiefs of the tribe that Her Majesty has heard with much satisfaction of their faithful conduct in declining to take up arms with the Sioux Indians, and has been much gratified by this evidence of their loyalty and attachment. You will further apprise them that the Great Mother desires to assure them that she has always taken, and will continue to take, a lively interest in all that concerns their welfare and trusts that nothing may at any time occur to disturb the friendly relations between her Indians and her white subjects."

The spring of 1876 saw more cattle and horses brought into Alberta from Montana. Jim Christy and George Emerson came with small separate herds. The horses — Christy's — were first to be offered for sale or trade. He found a good market among the white settlers and police, who paid on an average $100 per head. The horses were about 15½ hands, tough and used to ranging out in the winter, the best ever procured for police purposes. George Emerson, an old Hudson's Bay Company ex-employee of 1869, brought in the cows which he readily sold to the settlers beginning farming and stock-raising in southern Alberta. About 30 men left the force this spring, many locating land with their North-West Mounted Police scrip in the Macleod and Pincher Creek districts. Considerable business was done at Macleod this year. I. G. Baker & Company shipped 40,000 buffalo robes and wolf skins, the proceeds of their winter's trade there and at Calgary. W. F. Parker, ex-sergeant of the police, also took up a farm near Macleod and purchased a herd of cattle from J. Healy at Whoop-up. A French-Canadian named Beaupre located at Pincher Creek, and Jim Votier, an old trader, near Fish Creek. This year may be said to have seen the beginning of farming and stock-raising in today's southern Alberta.

A report of the Assistant Commissioner regarding the killing of the buffalo reads:

"The country between Cypress Hills and the Rocky Mountains, which has hitherto been claimed by the Blackfeet as their hunting ground, has this year been encroached upon by other Indians and half-breeds, causing much irritation among the Blackfeet, who have called upon the police to protect them in maintaining their rights to their territory, saying that if they were not restrained by the presence of the police they would make war upon the intruders. The correspondence on this subject has been submitted to the Lieutenant-Governor of the North-West Territories in order that it may receive the consid-

Crowfoot, a famous Blackfoot chief, and a Blackfoot camp in 1883. With the disappearance of the buffalo, the Blackfoot and other tribes were reduced to near starvation, living on handouts from the government. Despite this hardship, Crowfoot remained loyal to the whites who had destroyed their way of life.

eration of the North-West Council in connection with the adoption of rules for hunting and for preserving the buffalo from extinction."

A law was passed by the North-West Council prohibiting the killing of buffalo calves, but it was never more than a dead letter, being found impossible to enforce. The multitudinous duties of the police, the vastness of the country, and the thousands of Indians continually engaged in hunting made such a law absurd on the face of it.

The foundation of what was to become the coal city of Lethbridge was laid when an old miner named Nick Sheran opened the first seam. For several years he supplied the police at Fort Macleod with coal hauled by bull teams and displacing wood as fuel. Others secured it at the mine mouth for $3 per ton. He also loaded any bull teams returning empty to Fort Benton, and found there a ready market. Sheran worked his mine for several years and made considerable money. He was drowned in the Old Man's River while bathing.

Toward the end of the bitter winter of 1875-6, the Reverend George McDougall, with his sons John and David, came down from Morley to secure a supply of buffalo meat and camped on Nose Creek north of Fort Calgary. The minister left camp alone one morning to hunt. A blizzard came up during the day and he never returned. The police searched for several days and picked up the horse, but it was a week before the body was recovered. The minister had let his mount go, wandered round on foot and succumbed to the intense cold. This was the first death at Calgary since the arrival of the police and it cast a shadow over the New Year.

Sergeant-Major Clyde and myself, with Mr. Bunn of the Hudson's Bay Company, had a narrow escape while looking for Mr. McDougall. The weather had turned quite mild after a period of the severest cold. We were 10 miles up the Bow River, without overcoats or moccasins, when one of the sudden changes peculiar to the region occurred.

From bright sunshine and a summer-like western breeze, the wind swung swiftly to the north and a fierce blizzard swept down upon us. We rode for our lives, but it became so thick that we missed the fort. However, we struck the river a mile or so above it and luckily recognized the locality. We arrived at the fort chilled to the bone. A very little more exposure would have made our case much worse. As it was we were all nipped, my boots were frozen stiff and feeling only returned to my feet after I had held them for a long time in a basin of snow. But the lesson was not lost upon us. We were careful ever afterwards not to take such chances, however alluring the weather.

CHAPTER NINE

The Blackfoot Treaty of 1877

With good reason, the assembly of 7,000 Indians caused the Mounties great uneasiness.

In 1877 the Comptroller of the North-West Mounted Police reported as follows:

"In consequence of the manner in which the Blackfeet Indians had scattered over the plain during the early winter and spring, it was found impossible until the month of August to communicate to them the message expressing Her Majesty's appreciation of their conduct in rejecting the overtures from the Sioux Indians of the United States to join in a war of extermination against the white population. Assistant Commissioner Irvine, who conveyed the message to the Indians, reports that Her Majesty's expression of approval was received by them with the liveliest feeling of satisfaction and gratitude. They expressed their unaltered loyalty to the British Crown, and repeated their willingness to fight in its defence if they were ever required to do so. At the time of these expressions of loyalty from the Blackfeet, the United States newspapers were announcing the probability of the Northern Indians, who were represented as being ready for revolt, joining Sitting Bull and other hostiles in a devastating Indian War."

In the spring of 1877, the Commissioner received word at Fort Macleod that the government intended that summer to make a treaty with the Blackfeet and other tribes of plains Indians, giving them reservations and such allowances as might be deemed necessary. Governor Laird would proceed to Fort Macleod from Battleford, the treaty would be negotiated at the Blackfoot Crossing about 90 miles from Fort Macleod, and all tribes coming under that treaty were at once to be notified.

This was no easy task since the Indians were widely scattered, hunting buffalo. Not until July was all in readiness and the ground laid out at the Crossing for the majority of the two troops stationed at Macleod and Calgary to proceed with their transport and camp equipage. Inspector Crozier had charge of the preparations.

I left Calgary with a detachment of F troop for the Crossing on September 14, and on arriving found most of the Indians already collected. The valley at the Blackfoot Crossing on the south side of the Bow River where the treaty was held is about three miles long by one wide, with plenty of timber along the river and good feed for horses on the hills to the south and in the valley itself. There must have been at least 1,000 lodges in camps on both sides of the river. They were plentifully supplied with meat, having only just left a large buffalo herd down the stream to the east. Their horses, herded day and night, covered the uplands to the north and south of the camp in thousands.

It was a stirring and picturesque scene: great bands of grazing horses, the mounted warriors threading their way among them, and, as far as the eye could reach, white Indian lodges glimmering among the trees along the river bottom. By night the valley echoed to the dismal howling of the camp's curs, and from sun to sun drums boomed from the tents. Dancing, feasting, conjuring, incantations over the sick, prayers for success in the hunt or in war — all went to form a panorama of wild life vastly novel and entertaining, and seen but once. Never before had such a concourse of Indians assembled on Canada's western plains; never had the tribes appeared so contented and prosperous.

The tribes represented were Blackfeet, Bloods, Piegans, Sarcees, and Stonies. Many Cree had been drawn by curiosity to the treaty ground, as well as half-breeds who hoped to derive some gain from the annuities to be paid the Indians. Traders from both the north and south displayed their stocks in tents, while white men from Montana had brought in bands of horses for trade. A fair-sized horse fast enough to run buffalo would always fetch a good price from the Indians.

I. G. Baker & Company and T. C. Powers were both occupying large hastily-built stores with log walls and canvas roofs, well stocked with goods. The Hudson's Bay Company was also represented. Chief Factor Hardisty and his family had come down from Edmonton, and his brothers-in-law, the Reverend John and David McDougall, from Morley, the former to act as interpreter and adviser to the Stony Indians. They camped apart from the Blackfeet, with whom they were not on very good terms. Governor Laird, with the police commissioner, Colonel Macleod, and police escort of 60 men, arrived from Macleod after some days and went into camp. A large council tent was also erected.

Several days were occupied in preliminaries and in discussions between the different chiefs and officers and the Governor. More than once it looked as if all chance of concluding a treaty would have to be abandoned, the Indians threatening to leave the ground. The chief problem was old jealousies existing not only between different tribes but among individuals. The adjustment of these matters called for the exercise of tact and diplomacy, with the patience shown by the Commissioners beyond all praise. After a week of parleying and negotiations, however, the terms were finally agreed upon. The following day, September 22, 1877, was set for the signing of the treaty.

The main provisions included a reserve big enough to allow one square mile for each family of five, and in the same proportion for larger or smaller families; an immediate cash payment of $12 for every man, woman and child of the families at the ceremony; an annual payment of $25 to each Chief, $16 to each Minor Chief or Councillor, not to exceed 16 Minor Chiefs to the Blackfoot, Piegan and Blood Indians, four to the Sarcee band and five Councillors to the Stony band. In addition, $5 was to paid to every other Indian, regardless of age.

Other provisions included $2,000 a year for ammunition and a suit of clothes every three years, during their term of office, to each Head Chief and Minor Chief, and each Chief and Councillor. Teachers would be provided, as well as cattle, farm equipment and seed for "...the encouragement of the practice of agriculture among the Indians."

The number of Indians paid at the treaty was 4,824 who received $58,157. The Governor complimented the policemen for their laudable efforts in bringing the negotiations to a successful conclusion. He also noted:

"On Sunday the Indians fought a sham battle on horseback. They wore only the breech-cloths. They fired off their rifles and sent the bullets whistling past the spectators in such close proximity as to create most unpleasant feelings. I was heartily glad when they defiled past singly on the way back to their lodges and the last of their unearthly yells died away in the distance.

"Monday, Tuesday, and Wednesday were occupied in paying off the different tribes. They were paid by Inspector Winder, Sub-Inspector Denny, and Sub-Inspector Antrobus, each assisted by a constable of the force. It was hard work to find out the correct number of each family. Many after receiving their money would return to say that they had made a wrong count. One would discover that he had another wife, another two more children, and others that they had blind mothers and lame sisters. In some cases they wanted to be paid for the babies that were expected to come soon...."

The Blackfeet, Bloods, and Sarcees first took a reserve in

common on both sides of the Bow River for many miles above and below Blackfoot Crossing. Their relations were not amicable. Next year the Bloods were transferred to a new location on the Belly River and the Sarcees to the Elbow River above Calgary. The Blackfeet remained at the Crossing. The Piegans had located in the Porcupine Hills above Macleod, and the Stonies at Morley.

The sham battle given by the Blackfeet at the treaty was, as the Governor stated in his report, to say the least, unpleasant. He was not told of the uneasy feeling prevailing. The Indians had been in a state of excitement all the morning. While we were attending to our duties, 5-600 mounted warriors, stripped with the exception of a blanket round the loins and in war-paint and feather head-dresses, staged a mounted war-dance round our camp. These men, armed with loaded Winchesters and on the dead run, circled the tents, their rifles exploding and the bullets whistling over our heads. Their blood-curdling whoops accentuated the unpleasantness.

They were only half in fun. Had fear been shown by us the sham battle might easily have become one of grim earnestness. We went on quietly with our duties, however, and after a time the braves tired of their warlike demonstration and returned to their camps. Nevertheless this caused us, while it lasted, considerable uneasiness. Many of the Indians, we knew, were dissatisfied that a treaty had been made at all. A few unruly spirits might in a reckless moment have started a massacre, out of which none of our small party could have escaped.

The payments commenced on Tuesday. The money had been brought by I. G. Baker & Company from Fort Benton in both American and Canadian bills in denominations from $1 to $20. As the Indians knew nothing about money, it was most difficult to make them understand values of the different bills. Tickets were issued to each head of a family, with his name and number of men, women, and children paid, these tickets to be presented at the next payment. It was very difficult to obtain the names and numbers in each family. The Indians themselves, then and for many years afterwards, would not tell their own names. It was generally necessary to ask a second Indian the name of the first.

They also had some superstition about giving their numbers which made our work long and arduous and called for the exercise of much patience. The payments were made by the police officers and required nearly a week. But at last all details were satisfactorily concluded and our success celebrated in a dinner that night in the officers' mess-tent.

The traders were given a week from the conclusion of the payments to finish trading. The police, of course, remained to

Crowfoot addressing North-West Territories Lieutenant-Governor David Laird and Commissioner Macleod at the signing of Treaty Number 7 on September 22, 1877.

see that all went on quietly and also to protect the Indians. Money was new to them and some of the trading gentry were not above cheating. An Indian would come to us to count his change after the purchase of a horse or article. Frequently we found that he had been given the labels off fruit jars or cans as money, being none the wiser. We had then to hunt up the culprit and deal with him. The money taken in by the traders at this treaty was the foundation of wealth for many of them, particularly those dealing in horses.

The Indians built a medicine lodge before they broke up and made braves, at that time an annual custom. Torture was always inflicted. Slits were cut in the flesh of chest or shoulders, and wooden cleats inserted under the raised muscles. From these, rawhide lines ran to the top of the medicine pole. The Indian, putting his weight against them, danced round the pole until the muscles broke under the strain and released him. Or a buffalo skull might be hung from his back while he danced until freed. Or he might be tied to a horse and dragged. Great endurance was often shown, and the greater the fortitude displayed, the higher became the standing of the brave in the tribe.

Owing to the presence in Canada of their enemies, the American Sioux, against whom they were planning to send war parties, the making of braves was popular among the Blackfeet at the time of the treaty negotiations.

CHAPTER TEN

After the Custer Massacre

The Sioux cross into Canada, carrying guns, clothing and scalps from over 200 U.S. cavalrymen killed at the Little Bighorn River.

The weather turned cold, and a considerable fall of snow made life under canvas far from comfortable before we left the Blackfoot Crossing. Toward the end of the last week, word came that the American Government was sending General Terry as commissioner to meet with Sitting Bull at Fort Walsh for his surrender to the United States. The Sioux chief had crossed over with many thousands of his followers into Canada after the annihilation by the Indians, on the Little Big Horn in Montana, of General Custer and his command, and the subsequent pursuit by General Miles and his army. Colonel Macleod was to proceed immediately to Fort Walsh with a suitable escort to meet General Terry at the boundary and represent the Canadian Government.

A portion of Lieutenant-Colonel Macleod's recommendation to Prime Minister Alexander Mackenzie is as follows:

"I am of the opinion that the presence of these United States Sioux in our territory is a matter of very grave importance. There is not much reliance to be placed on their promises and they have not been on friendly terms with the Blackfeet or Crees for years back. The Blackfeet, I know, are anxious about the invasion of their country. They say that before our arrival they were always able to keep them out, but they now wish to be friends so long as they keep away. While at Swan River I heard that the Crees are very suspicious of the Sioux who had crossed the Line. I think therefore that an attempt should be made at once to get these Indians — who are now in a very impoverished condition — to re-cross to the United States side. The longer it is delayed the more difficult it will be to accomplish."

The following extract from a letter to Colonel Macleod from

the Honorable David Mills, Minister of the Interior at Ottawa, August 24, 1877, informs him of the appointment of a commission by the United States Government to interview Sitting Bull:

"The Government are most anxious that the United States commissioners should succeed in inducing the hostile Sioux who have come into our territory to return again to the United States. It is feared that should they remain in Canada they will be drawn into hostile conflict with our own Indians, that on going upon the hunting grounds of the Blackfeet and Assiniboines, or Crees, they will excite the opposition and resentment of these tribes, and that ultimately, from a failure of the means of subsistence and from other causes, they will become a very considerable expense to the Government of Canada. It is not at all improbable that they may also be disposed to make hostile incursions into the United States and in this way become a source of international trouble.

"These Indians while engaged in hostilities with the United States were reported to be guilty of acts of such barbarous cruelty that should they again return for the purpose of scalping women and children, their conduct would not fail to excite the indignation of the Government and people of the United States against this country. It is, therefore, important that you should use your influence to promote as far as you well can the object of the United States commissioners in securing the return of these Indians to their own reservations."

The United States commissioners arrived at the boundary line in the middle of October. General Terry and General McNeill were accompanied by their staff, also a strong escort of United States cavalry. We met them with 25 men. It was a continual surprise to the American officers with what a handful we managed to control and keep quiet the thousands of the most warlike Indians on the continent, there being only about 60 men all told at Fort Walsh.

The American cavalry escort remained in camp at the Line near the Sweet Grass Hills, while we escorted General Terry and staff to Fort Walsh. The Sioux, several thousand strong, were camped not far from the fort when we arrived. Because they were far from being in a peaceable mood, the responsibility for the safety of the American officers rested heavily on the shoulders of the small police detachment.

The following day was set for the interview. That night the Sioux warriors held a war-dance outside the fort and several of us, with our Sioux interpreter, went to see it. The Indians in their war-paint danced round the fire, hideously ornamented and painted. One chief was most conspicuous. He was naked except for the breech-cloth round his middle, his body black-

D Division of the NWMP at Fort Calgary in 1883. Had trouble started with the Sioux, the Mounties would have been greatly outnumbered.

ened and ribs painted white, while his face was that of a devil. He wore a long feather head-dress and a pair of buffalo horns on each side of his head. From his coup-stick (a long rod wrapped with raw-hide, an oblong stone at the end), hung many scalp locks. As he recounted his deeds of valour he pointed to these grizzly trophies and told how he had used this stick upon American soldiers at the Custer fight, knocking them off their horses and then dispatching them.

This Indian was Rain-in-the-Face, who was credited with killing General Custer, against whom he had an old grudge. Rain-in-the-Face and others harangued the Indians, urging them to attack the fort and kill the American officers. It would be easy they said, to destroy the buildings and all in them. This army of savage warriors could most certainly have done it, but the older chiefs opposed them and spoke for peace. Where, they asked, would they go if they were at war with the whites on both sides of the boundary? In the end their wise counsel prevailed.

The Sioux camp was well off for food. The buffalo were near and meat was plentiful. Of tea and tobacco they also seemed to have a good supply. They were well armed, had quantities of ammunition and appeared content and disposed to remain quiet, at least for the winter.

After being searched for firearms, the following morning

the chiefs were admitted to the fort. In the orderly-room General Terry and his staff, with Colonel Macleod and the police officers, awaited them. The chiefs shook hands with our officers but haughtily ignored the Americans. General Terry then announced the terms of the United States Government if they chose to re-cross the border and surrender. They would be required to give up their arms and to leave their former homeland of the Dakotas for the Indian Territory in the south.

When he had finished, Colonel Macleod informed them that as trespassers on Canadian soil they could not look for assistance from the Queen's Government. They would not be forced to return to the United States, however, so long as they were peaceable and obeyed the laws.

Sitting Bull was spokesman for the Indians. He began to recount their grievances but was at once checked. Such a recital might easily start trouble. They were told to answer briefly "Yes" or "No" whether they would surrender. They then refused the terms of the United States Commissioners and begged to be allowed to remain in Canada. After some more talk the council closed and the Indians returned to their camp.

That afternoon a detachment of police escorted General Terry's party back to the boundary. The Americans thoroughly appreciated the work we did for them and again expressed astonishment that so small a force could control such a vast country and the thousands of warlike red men who roamed its plains and valleys. It was a great relief to us to see them safely over the Line and away. Our responsibility was heavy. A constant watch was necessary to anticipate any hostile move and we had all felt uneasy.

Except for scalps, clothing, and guns, the Sioux had few trophies from the Custer fight. General Custer's watch was secured and sent to Mrs. Custer. His horses had been drowned while crossing the Missouri River. The clothing was of little use to the Indians, whose dress was limited to breech-clout and buffalo robe. They were a splendid-looking lot of warriors and without doubt the wildest and most warlike on the continent. They remained on the Canadian side, camped near Wood Mountain, until 1882 when, the buffalo having disappeared, they were forced to surrender to the American Government. During their stay in Canada they were the cause of some trouble and much anxiety. It was a matter for congratulation that so small a body as was the force in those early days were able to hold them in check, especially since this was only one of countless duties it was called upon to perform in all parts of the North-West Territories.

A troop under canvas at Fort Walsh in 1879. From 1878 to 1882 the post became the force's headquarters but declined in importance when the Sioux returned to the U.S.

CHAPTER ELEVEN

First Mountie to be Murdered

Constable Marmaduke Grayburn is shot from behind, then the prime suspect was acquitted for lack of evidence.

In August 1879 occurred the first round-up in southern Alberta, 16 cattle owners taking part. Many of these men in the course of years made money in the cattle business, owning individually thousands of range cattle and horses and leasing large tracts of land from the government. They were the pioneers of what became the great stock industry of southern Alberta.

The mail route of the southern half of the Territories had not been changed since the building of Fort Macleod and Fort Walsh. There were no post offices between the Rocky Mountains and the western boundary of Manitoba, at least 750 miles. Letters were posted in the Mounted Police orderly rooms at Calgary, Macleod, Walsh and Wood Mountain, with United States postage stamps attached, as the nearest post offices were in American territory.

The orderly-room clerks sorted and made up the mails, which were carried to their destinations by contract with the Mounted Police. The service was fortnightly, from Fort Macleod and Calgary to Fort Walsh, thence to Benton, in the years 1879 to 1880, and the mail was chiefly official. In the north, mail was carried by contract with the Post Office Department and picked up at Hudson's Bay Company and police posts on the way.

Recruits for the force came in via Benton and there was much travel between the North-West Territories and points in Montana. Although at that time Montana Territory had a considerable white population, it was made up in the main of cattle ranchers, miners, gamblers, traders, adventurers, and "bad" men who came and went. Lawlessness was rife and vigilance committees were formed, which dealt out summary justice to the tough element. Lynchings were frequent. It was said 40 men were hanged by these committees for horse-stealing, murder, and other crimes in the town of Benton and vicinity in less than three years.

In 1879 the pay of the force was reduced to 50 cents a day. Other changes were made. Inspectors were to be known as superintendents, sub-inspectors as inspectors, while military rank of the non-commissioned officers was confirmed by law. A chief constable was a sergeant-major and a constable a sergeant.

The sale of whisky to Indians had by this time been practically stamped out, although occasional instances cropped up of its being traded. But much liquor still found its way into the country for sale chiefly to settlers and to whites. Some now and then was disposed of even at a police post. The poorest quality, costing in Benton \$2 to \$3 a gallon, sold readily at Macleod or other posts for \$10 per bottle. The vendors took great chances, penalties being severe.

Fines ranged up to \$300 for a third offence, with confiscation of horses, wagons, and other outfit. But profits were so large that the traffic persisted all through the early years of prohibition in the Territories. It was impossible completely to eliminate the evil. Liquor was always procurable at a high price in any of the small towns or settlements in spite of the constant patrol of the Boundary Line and the close watch kept on all suspected traders.

At Fort Macleod in the old days the vilest concoctions were sold, the favourite Jamaica ginger. A six-ounce bottle, compounded of alcohol and a few drops of ginger extract, cost \$1. Red ink, Florida water, eau-de-Cologne and many other alcoholic fluids were used as beverages. Liquor permits for 2½ gallons were granted to persons recommended to the Lieutenant-Governor. The liquor was ostensibly for medical purposes, but the permit system was much abused. Men detected with quantities of liquor in their possession had permits to cover it in the names of different individuals and were therefore safe from arrest or prosecution. Gambling was openly practised, there being no law against it.

Until 1878, the police had drawn upon the buffalo for its meat supply. But in that year contracts were made with I. G. Baker & Company to furnish the force with domestic beef. The firm drove in herds of range cattle and opened butcher shops at the various posts. The contract price for the meat was 14 cents per pound and they made enormous profits, the cattle costing them in Montana an average of around \$20 per head.

Since our arrival in the Territories in 1874, a number had died from one cause or another, but no man of the force had

Constable Grayburn's memorial on the creek where he was murdered. The inscription reads: "This monument was erected by his comrades . . . as a token of the esteem in which they held him."

Star Child, top right, was tried for the murder but the jury, after deliberating for 24 hours, found him not guilty.

been killed or molested by an Indian. But the time came when this unclouded record was to be broken. In October 1879 a policeman was deliberately murdered near Fort Walsh. Four constables and a non-commissioned officer, in charge of the police horse herd, were in camp some three miles from the post. During the day one man was continually on herd; at night the horses were driven in to the fort and stabled. At the time of the murder, some Blood Indians who made themselves obnoxious by continual prowling and begging were in camp not far from the police tents. On the fateful morning Constable Grayburn left camp to take his turn on herd and was followed by a Blood named Star Child. This Indian was a vicious character who had given much trouble to the police, and Grayburn had shortly before had words with him.

When the time came for Grayburn to be relieved he did not return to camp. Search was immediately made for him. Hanging from a bush about a mile away, his companions found his cap and, in the snow nearby, stains of blood. At the bottom of a gully a little farther on the searchers came upon his body, a bullet hole in the back of the head. His horse, tied by the halter shank, lay dead at the foot of a tree, also shot.

Word of the tragedy was sent to the fort and the body removed. A party was dispatched to make a thorough search of the Blood camp, suspicion centering on Star Child. But the Indian could not be found. It was subsequently learned that he had escaped to Montana.

Efforts were made unsuccessfully to extradite him, but in 1881 he returned to the Blood camp near Fort Macleod. After repeatedly escaping arrest by his alertness, he was captured. He was tried at Macleod for murder. Although morally certain of his guilt, in the absence of any evidence the jury could do nothing but bring in a verdict of acquittal. A year or two later Star Child was arrested for horse stealing. This time he was less fortunate. He received a sentence of five years in Manitoba penitentiary and died before completing his term.

In the fall and winter of 1879 the Canadian Indians were returning from the American side. But the buffalo — except for a few scattered animals found on rare occasions up to 1884 between Wood Mountain and Battleford — were gone from the North-West Territories. The returning Indians were in dire distress and flocked to the different police posts for assistance. Mr. Dewdney, the Indian Commissioner, had arranged with I. G. Baker & Company to furnish flour and beef cattle for the relief of Indians. But the amount was limited. When thousands of destitute turned to the Government in their only hope of succour, the resources of the police were taxed to the utmost.

As soon as possible they were sent to their reserves and men were engaged by the Indian Department to look after them, but this could not be done until 1880. In the meantime their supervision fell upon the shoulders of the police. A most trying task it proved. Complaints of cattle-killing, calling almost daily for investigations, combined with the multitude of their other duties, gave the force little rest.

At Fort Calgary, where I commanded, as the summer advanced matters became serious. The Blackfeet were actually starving. Had I not taken the responsibility of coming to their relief, an outbreak must certainly have occurred. It was pitiable to see parties of the less impoverished bringing their weakened fellows, some mere skeletons, to Fort Calgary for food. Some even ate grass along the road.

I have seen them when a steer was shot rush on the animal with their knives before it had ceased kicking, cut away the flesh and, maddened by hunger, devour it raw. The Blackfeet were most grateful for the succour extended to them at this critical time. I found in after years when acting as their agent that to their recollection of this incident I owed much of my success in dealing with them in more than one ticklish situation.

Following is a copy of my report to Colonel Macleod from Fort Calgary on July 5, 1879:

"As Mr. Merret leaves this fort to-day to proceed via the Crossing to Fort Macleod, I have the honour to report how the Indians are situated at this post and the Blackfoot Crossing, and the action I have taken in the matter of feeding them. On the arrival of word from the Crossing that there were nearly two hundred lodges there starving and waiting for supplies, I immediately despatched S. C. Christie to Fort Macleod, with a letter to you stating the condition of the Indians, and asking permission to purchase beef for them, but since that time the Indians have been coming in here in hundreds, always headed by a chief, for food, as they are actually dying of starvation. (I have already heard of twenty-one cases of death.) As they are and have been getting no assistance from any post, I took upon myself the responsibility of purchasing and issuing beef to them. For the last three days I have been obliged to issue beef at the rate of two thousand pounds per diem. I have advised the Indians not to move their camp up here from the Crossing, as I expected you would have been at Fort Macleod when Constable Christie arrived there, and that some of the Indian cattle would be sent to the Indians at the Crossing. I have told them all that as soon as you arrived at Macleod provisions would be sent to them, and in the meantime I would supply them with meat, which I have done, and am now doing. Until assistance arrives from Fort Macleod I can keep them in meat the way I am doing for a week or two, but of course the expense will be great. I am buying cattle from Mr. Emerson at the post at seven cents per pound. There is no doubt whatever that if I had not fed them, and do not continue to feed them, they will take the matter into their own hands and help themselves.

"Crowfoot sent up word yesterday asking me to go down and talk to them in their distress. It is utterly impossible for me to leave here until the Blackfeet receive assistance from some other post. Crowfoot himself, I think, will be here to-morrow. All the other chiefs have been in with the exception of Three Bulls, who is at Cypress. The Blackfeet are utterly destitute, there being no buffalo in the country. I have had to send out meat to parties on their way in, who were eating grass to keep themselves alive. The rush is not quite so great as it was, as I have established some order in the going and coming. Every party that comes in is headed by a chief, who sends a man some hours ahead to notify me of their coming so that I can have meat ready for them. I am keeping careful note of what I issue, and to whom, and in what quantity. I am paying the men from whom I purchase beef by voucher on I. G. Baker & Company. I am nearly out of flour, and can issue no more without running myself short. I am not only feeding the Blackfeet, but also the Sarcees and Stonies and some half-breeds."

I had received orders from Mr. Dewdney, Indian Commissioner, in the spring not to provide rations for the Indians at Calgary. But such a state of affairs as I have described was not apprehended. Not long afterwards, I received a letter from the Indian Commissioner thanking me for the action I had taken.

Soon after this, cattle and flour were purchased in large quantities and sent to the reserves, men were engaged as butchers and the police went to see that a fair issue of rations was made. Next year regular farm instructors were appointed and in 1880 Norman Macleod, brother of the Commissioner, was named first Indian Agent over the whole treaty. On his resignation in 1882, I was offered and accepted the position, resigning my commission in the force for the purpose.

For a year or two the Indians continued to leave their reserves in large numbers in search of the vanished buffalo. It was hard to make them believe that they were gone forever. For years they believed they would reappear. They had a legend that the buffalo came originally from a hole in the ground in the center of a lake in the north and that on the advent of the whites they had re-entered it and would ultimately re-emerge. L. V. Kelly in his book, *The Rangemen*, says:

"Across the boundary the slaughter of the hemmed-up buffalo continued, and the white and red hunters made huge kills. One hundred thousand buffalo robes were sold out of the Yellowstone valley from the winter hunt of 1880 and 1881, but never again would there be such a shipment, for the herds of millions had now dwindled to a few thousands, and the day of the buffalo was gone."

In 1882 Sitting Bull and his hostile following were forced by the disappearance of the buffalo to surrender at Fort Buford on the Missouri River to the United States authorities, relieving us of endless responsibility and trouble. He was subsequently shot to death by Indian police of his own tribe. A perpetual supervision over them had been necessary since their arrival in 1876. The force at Wood Mountain, which had most to do with the Sioux, with Major Crozier in command, consisted of less than 50 men behind a flimsy wooden stockade that a war-party of Sioux could have taken in an hour.

The Blackfeet were frequent callers at our posts when near there, and individual hunters roamed the country on the lookout for any shaggy stragglers that might remain. A starving Blood Indian appeared at Wood Mountain making for the post and ran upon the Sioux. Instantly, they were in pursuit of their solitary enemy like a pack of hounds.

The Blood evaded them by hiding in the brush and managed to get into the fort at night, where he was promised protection. The Sioux on learning this flocked to the fort in hundreds, to find the gates closed against them. They demanded the surrender of the Blood, threatening if their request was refused to burn the fort and kill all behind its walls.

Preparations were made for defence and Superintendent Crozier went to the gate to parley with Sitting Bull. For an hour he argued with the chief. Then when Sitting Bull suddenly attempted to force his way past him into the fort, the major seized the Sioux by the shoulders and flung him out. An immediate attack was anticipated. But the firmness shown by the police daunted even these fierce redskins. They returned to their camp sullen and vowing vengeance. That night the Blood was smuggled out, mounted on a good horse and sent on his way. He reached Fort Walsh with his scalp intact, thanks to the courage of the Wood Mountain detachment and their commander.

In November 1880 Lieutenant-Colonel Macleod resigned from the force and the Assistant Commissioner, Lieutenant-Colonel Irvine, succeeded him. Colonel Macleod did not leave the country, however. Until 1886 he was stipendiary magistrate and that year was appointed judge.

During the winter of 1879 word was received at Fort Walsh

Sioux Chief Sitting Bull and Superintendent L. Crozier. When the Chief tried to force his way into Wood Mountain, Crozier threw him out.

East End Detachment in 1878. The post was one of several new ones established along the border to closely watch the unwelcome Sioux, traditional enemies of many Canadian tribes.

that the Indian Star Child (suspected, as has been related, of the murder of Constable Grayburn), was in an Indian camp south of Fort Benton. I was given orders to proceed there and try to arrange with the Benton sheriff to have the suspect delivered to us at the boundary. I was instructed to offer up to $500 for this purpose.

I rode into Benton in the spring of 1880. Unfortunately, the sum asked by Sheriff Healy for delivery of the Indian was out of my power to pay. This was my first visit to Fort Benton. I found it a busy place of some 1,000, at the head of navigation on the Missouri. A portion of the old fort, built of unbaked adobe bricks, still stood. There were handsome residences and business blocks. It was what was called a wide-open town. Water Street, facing the river, was lined with gambling houses, liquor saloons, and dance halls, the sidewalk and street strewn with playing cards, thrown out as the easiest way of getting rid of them.

By 1881 the force at Calgary had been reduced. The Indians were getting rations on their reserves and it was the intention to move most of the men to Forts Walsh and Macleod.

The Indians still looked for buffalo where none existed and the Blackfeet lodges were at or near the Crossing. A large camp of Crees arrived from the north and camped not far away. The two tribes were far from friendly; in fact, word reached Calgary that a Cree had been killed during the summer by a Blackfoot and that the Crees were about to attack the Blackfoot camp to avenge his death. I therefore started for that point with what men could be spared, which was six, including Corporal G. C. King and interpreter Munro.

An American officer, Captain Williams, who had come from Montana after some army mules taken by deserters from his regiment, had been staying with me for a short time. He asked permission to accompany us to the Crossing and I was glad of his company. We rode light, with a spring wagon for bedding and provisions, and made the Crossing late that night. In the morning we found a Blackfoot camp of about 1,000 on the edge of the bluff overlooking the river. The Cree camp, nearly equal in size, was about three miles distant.

The Blackfoot chiefs came down to see me, bringing many complaints against the Crees. I asked if it was true that a Cree had been killed. They admitted the killing, but alleged provocation. I demanded they give up the slayer, but found that he had left the camp the day after the occurrence and gone no one knew where. I then told them to pitch a large lodge somewhere between their camp and that of the Crees. Meanwhile, I would go over to the Cree camp and try to persuade their chiefs to also promised to talk reasonably and endeavour to settle their differences.

I rode with the interpreter to the Cree village, finding them more amenable than I had anticipated. In fact they were feeling far from comfortable. They were in Blackfoot country, a long way from their friends and more likely to be attacked by their hereditary enemies than to attack them. They were much incensed, however, over the killing of one of their number. But at last they consented to accept a payment from the Blackfeet in settlement and agreed to meet their former foes next day in council. When the matter was adjusted they would move camp to the Cypress Hills, as advised.

This reply, which I brought to the Blackfeet, satisfied them. I found that in my absence they had brought a supply of dried meat and put up a lodge for us. We had no tent and this was most welcome. It was intended as evidence of great friendliness on their part.

Next morning, with the interpreter and Captain Williams, I went to the Blackfoot camp and was shown the tent pitched for the council. We seated ourselves at the head of it and awaited the arrival of the chiefs. After a short interval the head Blackfoot chief, Crowfoot, arrived. With great ceremony he passed round the fire and shook hands with us, at the same time throwing down a fine dressed buffalo robe before me. I told the interpreter to tell them that I had not come to take presents but to settle the dispute between themselves and the Crees. Munro advised me to take the robe as it was given as a token of their good-will towards us. I therefore threw the robe behind me.

Soon afterwards no less than 33 more Cree and Blackfoot chiefs arrived. Each as he entered threw down a robe as Crowfoot had done. This was embarrassing as, having taken the first, I could not, without affronting the other chiefs, refuse the rest. I had, therefore, 34 robes piled at my back. A little later we felt grateful to the chiefs. We were short of bedding and the weather turned cold before we returned to Calgary. I distributed the robes among the men, who were delighted to get them.

Following a solemn smoke all round, I advised the Blackfeet to settle with the family of the slain Cree in the usual Indian fashion by payment of so many horses. For several hours, however, we were obliged to listen while they aired their grievances against each other. The talk at times was loud and heated, but in the end the opposing tribes came to an agreement. The Crees promised to move the following day and the Blackfeet to give up the murderer should he come into camp. I got them to shake hands all round.

After seeing the Crees out of camp we returned to our

lodges tired but well satisfied with the day's results. Our success in settling such matters among our Indians astonished Captain Williams. He said on his side of the Line it would have taken a regiment of cavalry and a war to have done what we accomplished with a handful of men. We remained at the Crossing for two days and saw the Crees well started on their way east before returning to Calgary.

In the fall of 1881 I left Calgary for Fort Walsh. Sergeant Johnston remained in charge of Fort Calgary, the only persons besides him being G. C. King, now manager of I. G. Baker & Company's store, and the Hudson's Bay Company trader, A. Fraser, and his man. I took with me all F troop with the exception of the Sergeant and after a few days at Macleod went on to Fort Walsh. While we were at Macleod a bad fire broke out which burned down the quartermaster's stores and some stables, causing considerable loss. The village of Macleod had not grown. Since much of it had slipped into the Old Man's River, the Commissioner had recommended that the fort be moved and rebuilt in a more secure situation.

NWMP officers at Fort Walsh in 1877. The author is standing at right in the back row.

CHAPTER TWELVE

Death in the Belly River

The policemen learn that the West's flooding rivers can be as dangerous as a winter blizzard.

In 1880 a few more settlers came in and several time-expired police also went into farming and stock raising. In 1881 the first Government leases were granted in southern Alberta — large tracts for 21-year periods at the nominal rent of one cent per acre. The Oxley Ranch Company, a group of rich English shareholders headed by Lord Lathom and Stavely Hill, was organized. On its 100,000-acre lease on Willow Creek were placed several thousand head of cattle. The Cochrane Company, under Senator Cochrane's direction, secured a large lease west of Calgary but later moved south of the Belly River. They brought from Montana 10,000 head of cattle. The Allans, of Allan Steamship fame, established themselves on High River under the name of the North-West Cattle or Bar U Company. Although most of these leases were granted late in 1880 or early in 1881, it was a year before the majority were in operation. All stock was purchased in Montana and, in general, experienced cattlemen were engaged in the south to manage these large concerns.

The summers of 1880 and 1881 were very wet, the rivers high, and the losses in the herds from Montana in crossing them quite heavy. At Macleod the river banks were continually crumbling, buildings were swept away, and it became apparent that to escape a like fate, the fort must soon be moved.

Captain Winder left the Mounted Police in 1881 to establish a store at Macleod and a ranch on Willow Creek. Fred Stimson came in to manage the Bar U ranch and Inspector James Walker left the force to take charge of the Cochrane ranch. He drove 12,000 head of cattle over from Montana in 1882 and ranged them some 20 miles west of Calgary. The following winter, which was unusually severe, the cattle died by hundreds and

In the early 1880s, multi-thousand-acre ranches were established in southern Alberta. Colonel Walker, opposite, left the force to manage the Cochrane Ranch, and in 1882 drove in 12,000 head of cattle from Montana. As ranching grew, one autumn cowboys rounded up 60,000 head from the region.

the river was polluted by the carcasses.

The route of the Canadian Pacific Railway had been changed and the road was under construction on its present location. Much disappointment was felt in the north over the change, the original survey crossing the Rockies over much lower and easier paths than that finally selected. There were various explanations, but no doubt pressure exerted by the wealthy cattle companies in the south was responsible for the shift. The Edmonton district had few settlers at the time and their representations counted for little against those of these powerful interests.

Colonel Macleod left Fort Walsh in the summer of 1880 to take up his duties as stipendiary magistrate at Fort Macleod. Having obtained a month's leave of absence, I took the opportunity of travelling with him. As he had a four-horse team and spring wagon, I was able to take my baggage and ride my troop horse. The Indian Agent's son, Norman, Guide Jerry Potts, and two constables were the others in the party.

Nothing happened until we reached the Belly River at Whoop-up. Here we found the stream very high and just managed to cross without swimming. After dinner we went on to Slide-out, the second crossing of the Belly. It was then about six o'clock. The Colonel and Jerry crossed the river on the ford without difficulty and I told Constable Hooley to drive in after him. When we were nearly half-way over, however, the Colonel called to me to return to the south bank, camp, and come over in the morning. He and Jerry were going on to Macleod, 9 miles north.

I was loath to do this, having made a good start, but orders were orders. We spent a most unpleasant night in the open. Mosquitoes were bad and sleep was almost impossible. Two of the horses, although hobbled, crossed the river and in the morning we could see them grazing on the other side.

A little after daylight I sent the driver, Hooley, over after them, instructing him to pay particular attention to the ford so that he would know his way when we started to cross. He got over safely and brought back the horses. I saw that the water was about breast-high on them and that the current was swift. Hooley pronounced the ford all right and said we would have no trouble in crossing. We loaded the wagon and drove in. A log house owned and occupied by two ex-police ranch men, Bell and Patterson, stood on the opposite side, but the hour being early they were still in bed.

We had reached the middle of the river when the lead team balked. I took the reins of the team, the driver attending to those of the wheelers. We succeeded in starting them all together, then I handed the reins back to the driver. But we had gone only a few steps when the leaders stopped a second time, swerving downstream and dragging the wheelers after them. Over went the wagon, throwing me among the floundering horses.

How I escaped injury is a miracle, but half-drowned I managed to reach the shore. Climbing the bank, I saw that young Macleod and Constable Stewart had both jumped and were also safe. Team and wagon were drifting down the center of the river. The driver had dropped the reins and was hanging to the side of the seat in water to his waist. The horses, entangled in the harness, were crazed with fear. The leaders had swung round and were frantically pawing on the team in the rear. The driver had completely lost his nerve.

"Mr. Denny," he called, "come and help me!"

I jumped into the river and swam towards him. I was nearing the wagon when suddenly it again turned over. Man, horses, and the vehicle disappeared. I swam over the spot and down the river for a quarter of a mile, but they did not reappear. My strength almost exhausted, I was forced to make for shore.

In the meantime the two young men had watched the tragic happening from the bank. I called out Bell and Patterson, borrowed two horses from them, and sent Stewart and Macleod to the fort for assistance. The ranchers and myself followed down the river and found the wagon attached to the four drowned horses on a sand-bar half a mile below the ford.

We were obliged to wait until a detail arrived with a boat aboard a wagon before we could reach the wreck. With much difficulty we disentangled the horses and brought harness and some recovered baggage ashore. We then went on down the river for several miles in hope of discovering the body of the driver, but as night came on we were reluctantly compelled to abandon the search.

Most of the baggage was never found but, oddly enough, not a thing belonging to Colonel Macleod was missing. Even his waistcoat, left on the driver's seat with his gold watch in the pocket, was recovered. I lost, among other things, a good part of my uniform, besides the three months' pay I had placed in the uniform case.

Poor Hooley's body was discovered, though not for nearly a month, about 12 miles from the scene of the accident. He was buried at Macleod with military honours. This was one of the many fatalities that occurred in the North-West in crossing the dangerous streams before the day of ferries and bridges. These mountain streams are most treacherous since the rapid currents cause frequent shifting of the sand bars. Where in one year a good ford might be found, in the next, swimming might be the only method of crossing from one bank to the other.

Not long after the Hooley tragedy, the dissatisfaction of the

Sarcee Indians over being placed on a common reserve with the Blackfeet came to a head when, 400 strong, they moved to Calgary and demanded to be fed there. The lone policeman at the time was Sergeant Johnston; the only other white men were G. C. King, manager of I. G. Baker & Company's store, Angus Fraser of the Hudson's Bay Company post, W. Smith and Walter James. The Sarcees, reduced in number through smallpox and warfare from a tribe of several thousand to one of perhaps 600, were the most difficult to handle of any of the plains Indians. They warred continually with other tribes, and though nominally allies of the Blackfeet, each camp distrusted the other.

The two stores were well supplied with goods and the Sarcees took advantage of the helplessness of the traders, demanding supplies and threatening if refused to help themselves. They beset the stores, shot off their guns and even built a fire in front of the Baker Company's place. Eventually they succeeded in so intimidating the men in charge that they were given what they asked. A messenger made a rapid ride to Macleod with the news and Inspector Crozier ordered me to proceed with a detail of eight men and a sergeant with all speed to Calgary. We were accompanied by the Indian agent. My instructions were to move the Sarcees from the place and punish any who had committed depredations. We arrived at Calgary on the second day, greatly to the relief of the few settlers in the locality. The Indians we found had up till then confined their hostile demonstrations to threats and firing guns inside the stores. The traders, however, to avert possibly more serious trouble, had been coerced into making them many presents.

The agent held a council in the fort. Upon the Sarcees refusing to return to the Crossing, he promised rations to them at Fort Macleod if they went there. This proposal they declined, demanding to be rationed at Calgary which, in the absence of cattle or other supplies there, was out of the question. The agent went on to Morley to visit the Stonies, leaving the Sarcees to us. For three days we could do nothing with them and the possibility of their attacking us necessitated a strong guard night and day. No doubt they would have done so had we not shown a bold front. However, on the third evening they consented to move next morning but, their horses being very poor, asked help to transport their tents and effects.

I promised them some carts, but at the same time told them that if they failed to move as agreed I would pull down and carry away their tents. This was a rather pretentious threat but it had to be made good. I engaged Sam Livingstone, a rancher up the Elbow River, to be on hand with a number of carts in the morning.

Early next day I went with all the men I could muster — 13

I believe — to the lodges. We found no sign of movement. I lined up the men, rifles loaded, on the camp's outskirts, then Sergeant Lauder and I commenced to pull down the tents.

The Indians had been sulking inside. They swarmed out like a nest of hornets and for a time things looked sultry. But they cooled off when they found themselves facing the row of rifles with determined men behind them. They began hurriedly to pack their goods into the carts. One shot, fired from behind a lodge still standing, came unpleasantly close to Sergeant Lauder. As the Indians were now busily preparing for the trail, we paid it only passing notice. By afternoon they were moving. We kept with them until next day and then rode on. They arrived four days later and for the next year drew rations at Macleod. A separate reservation was then allotted to them on Fish Creek, about 10 miles from Calgary.

A death that cast a gloom over us for a long time occurred this fall. Captain Clarke, the adjutant of the force, lately married, died at Fort Walsh of gastric fever. Walsh was always an unhealthy post and there were many deaths from the same cause during the few years it was occupied. Captain Clarke was the first officer we had lost since coming to the country and he was most popular. The surgeons of the force, Kittson and Kennedy, were both clever men, but their skill could not save him.

Settlements had now begun to dot the whole of the North-West Territories from the North Saskatchewan to the International Boundary. The country was being occupied, not rapidly but slowly and surely. Commissioner Irvine impressed upon the Government the necessity of increasing the force. His recommendation was approved and in 1881 the force was enlarged to 500 men. Since its organization in 1874 the strength had never exceeded 300. It had long been evident that there were too few for the work expected of them, especially since the Indians were now for the most part settled on reserves and the influx of settlers compelled a constant extension of police duties.

The force was divided among 13 posts: Fort Walsh, Qu'Appelle, Shoal Lake, Swan River, Fort Macleod, Blackfoot Crossing, Calgary, Pincher Creek, Blood Reserve, Battleford, Fort Saskatchewan, Prince Albert, and Wood Mountain. Because these various detachments were in most cases long distances apart, their number made the strength of each necessarily small. The increase, therefore, was most welcome. The large herds of stock now ranging the prairie were a standing temptation to the Indians and a constant watch was required to prevent wholesale cattle killing. The following extract from the Commissioner's report illustrates the conditions prevailing:

"Since the beginning of Treaty Seven in 1877, the Blackfeet,

Bloods, and Piegans have never been even temporarily assembled in Canadian territory up to their full strength. In 1877 it must be remembered that large quantities of buffalo were to be found in the country. The Indians were then self-supporting, almost rich, and certainly contented, and notwithstanding the fact that they were nothing less than savages, they were not dangerous. Now matters have completely changed. The savage nature alone remains, and they are partly dependent on the Government for a living. The yoke of dependence weighs somewhat heavily upon them. It is true, the policy of settling the Indians on reservations and instructing them in agricultural pursuits has been adopted, small bands have from time to time straggled in, found homes on the reserves and adopted the new mode of life, but the majority are fresh from south of the International Boundary Line, where they have been employed in hunting buffalo. It must be remembered that these Indians have led a lawless and roving life, that they have been accustomed from infancy to regard other men's cattle and horses as fair plunder and that the habits of a lifetime are not easy to unlearn. It is not natural to suppose that they will at once settle down to a quiet and humdrum life and devote themselves heart and soul to farming. Discontent may, in fact possibly will, break out and the spirit of unrest show itself, particularly among the young men, which, if not suppressed in time, will result in periodical raids on the cattle and horses of the settlers. This would in a short time lead to acts of retaliation and a serious outbreak would follow as a natural consequence.

"The number of Indians in the North-West Territories, all under the jurisdiction of the police, may be taken as twenty-seven thousand. The area of territory is some three hundred and seventy-five thousand square miles, almost equal to the area of France and Germany combined, or nearly twice that of Spain and Portugal."

In the late summer of 1881 the Crees and Assiniboines went south from Fort Walsh in the hope that there were still buffalo along the Missouri River. Although starving when they returned, it was with great difficulty that the majority were induced to go on the reserves near Fort Qu'Appelle. Big Bear, who had opposed the treaty, and his large following of Crees had for years been a source of trouble to the police at Fort Walsh. But in the spring of 1883 Big Bear signed at that place and moved with his band to the North Saskatchewan, only to create discord in that locality and join in the rebellion of 1885. The Commissioner states in his report: "Big Bear, who has I think unjustly borne a bad character, will make one of the best chiefs."

This prediction might well have been realized but age had

Indian camp at Fort Calgary in 1886. The crossed poles on the horse, a travois, was the traditional Indian way of hauling their tipis and other necessities. Dogs were also used, each hauling from 50 to 100 pounds.

stripped Big Bear of control over his band of miscreants, who murdered and pillaged at Frog Lake and Fort Pitt in 1885.

Fort Walsh was abandoned in 1883 and the force there under Inspector McIllree was moved to Fort Macleod. I left the Mounted Police in 1882 and at his request drove with Lieutenant-Governor Dewdney from Macleod to Fort Walsh to take charge as Indian Agent of the Crees and Assiniboines at that place. I succeeded after tedious negotiations in persuading them to move to their different reservations, the Crees to the north and the Assiniboines to the east.

Trouble had occurred at the Blackfoot Crossing. As a consequence, I was ordered by Mr. Dewdney to Fort Macleod to take over Treaty Number Seven which embraced the Blackfoot, Blood, Sarcee, and Stony Indians. In this post I was the successor of Norman Macleod who had resigned in 1882. The Blackfeet had only the previous year returned from a long sojourn across the Line. Little or no work had been done on the reserve, the Indians for the most part hanging round the Agency Buildings. The flour supply had sometimes run short during the winter and, remembering their experience in starving previous to going south, they were afraid of a recurrence. Two years spent at horse stealing and trading for whisky in Montana was not calculated to make the Blackfeet young men an altogether exemplary body, although they were more or less under control of the Soldiers' Lodge, organized while they were on the United States side.

CHAPTER THIRTEEN

Confrontation During CPR Construction

Bull Elk nearly starts a war, then Chief's Piapot and Long Man halt track laying on the Canadian Pacific Railway.

The Soldiers' Lodge was the cause of much trouble to the resident Indian Department employees. Guns had blazed in their proximity and one day a bullet whipped past a man employed by the butchers. It was fired by Bull Elk who declared that the man had sold him a beefhead and then delivered it to another Indian. Inspector Francis J. Dickens, son of the novelist Charles Dickens, was sent with a police detail from Macleod to arrest the offender. The Blackfeet, however, for the first time since the arrival of the police, offered resistance. Although the police were but a handful, vigorous efforts were made to take the Indian. He was arrested by Sergeant Howe and Constable Ashe. Then Constable Ashe was knocked down and to the accompaniment of exploding Blackfeet guns, Bull Elk was rescued. At this point proceedings were halted pending the arrival of reinforcements from Fort Macleod.

Superintendent Crozier with all available men — 20 — started immediately for the Crossing. He found the Indians upon his arrival greatly excited. Bull Elk, they declared heatedly, would not be given up. The situation was serious. Swift, uncompromising action was demanded if the prestige of the police among the Indians was not to be permanently impaired.

Superintendent Crozier informed Crowfoot that he intended to make the arrest and that unless Bull Elk was surrendered by the following day he would be taken by force. Meanwhile, one of the Indian Department buildings was converted into a temporary fort, with sacks of flour for breastworks. Precautions were taken against surprise. This prompt action overawed the Indians. Though many in number, they hesitated to provoke a crisis. Bull Elk was arrested without resistance next day and sent to Fort Macleod, tried by Judge Macleod and sentenced to a term in the guard-room.

This clash brought the police as near an actual conflict with the Indians, perhaps, as any that had occurred. The courage of officers and men averted what might easily have developed into such another war as those which, on the American side of the Line, have stained the soil with the blood of both red men and white.

In January 1883 the track-laying gangs on the Canadian Pacific Railway were only a few miles east of Maple Creek and by September trains were unloading passengers and freight in Calgary. Here a town had sprung up east of the Elbow River. Homesteaders and merchants were no longer dependent on the bull trains to deliver goods via Montana, as had been the case since 1874. Edmonton had still to be reached mainly by horse- or cattle-drawn vehicle over the old prairie trails, as had also for a time the territory to the south. But now all the freight was distributed from points on the Canadian Pacific Railway nearest the various outlying towns. The steel line, too, had opened to western ranchers markets in the east and the cattle industry was on the high road to success.

Over a period of years, survey parties had been at work exploring the various passes to determine the most feasible route through the mountains to the Pacific Coast. As in all great projects, many unrecorded deaths occurred in this pioneer force. Men perished in forest fires, in flooded rivers, in snow storms on the plains, and avalanches in the mountains. Some were murdered both by Indians and by white renegades. The building of this great trans-continental railway is a story by itself; a story of heartbreaking toil and hardship, of hunger and cold heroically endured; a story of gigantic enterprise carried through in the face of tremendous obstacles to a triumphant finish; and a story inseparably linked with the opening of Canada's great West.

While the actual laying of the track was in progress, thousands of men of almost all nationalities were employed. As a result, the work of the Mounted Police was greatly augmented. Among the laborers were many tough characters, a constant source of trouble. The greatest vigilance was necessary to prevent the sale to them of quantities of fiery liquor. Gamblers, thieves, bootleggers, and bad men generally were found close to the construction camps.

The Indians, too, became uneasy over this army of invasion and its peaceable purposes had to be explained to them. Although all of these duties fell to the Mounted Police, throughout these difficult times they maintained peace. The following letter from the general manager of the company, dated January 1, 1883, to the Commissioner of the Force, speaks for itself:

"Dear Sir,

"Our work of construction for the year 1882 has just closed, and I cannot permit the occasion to pass without acknowledging the obligations of the company to the North-West Mounted Police, whose zeal and industry in preventing traffic in liquor and preserving order along the line under construction have contributed so much to the successful prosecution of the work. Indeed, without the assistance of the officers and men of the splendid force under your command, it would have been impossible to have accomplished so much as we did. On no great work within my knowledge, where so many men have been employed, has such perfect order prevailed. On behalf of the company and of all the officers, I wish to return thanks and to acknowledge particularly our obligations to yourself and Major Walsh.

"W. C. Van Horne, General Manager."

The Crees and Assiniboines at the Cypress Hills and in the vicinity of construction at Maple Creek were most troublesome. Horses stolen by them from contractors were recovered by the police and the thieves were taken into custody and punished. But in many instances horse stealing attributed to Indians was really the work of white desperadoes following in the wake of construction. Fires, too, were the cause of much anxiety and did much damage, both on the prairie and in the mountains, destroying quantities of valuable timber.

One instance of the manner in which the police handled troublesome Indians during Canadian Pacific Railway construction involved a large Cree camp, of which Chiefs Piapot and Long Man were the heads. They sat down squarely on the line of construction and halted the advance. They announced that they were there to stay, that they would not allow the work to continue. The railway authorities appealed to the Lieutenant-Governor, who communicated with the nearest police post and asked them to move the Indians.

A sergeant and two men went to the camp and gave the Indians half an hour to move, promising should they fail to do so to pull down the tents. The Indians threatened and wasted some powder but showed no intention of moving. The three men proceeded calmly to flatten the tents, being apparently quite uninterested in any demonstrations by the Indians. This was enough. The camp came down in a hurry. Not a hand was lifted against the dauntless trio by the swarm of angry Crees surrounding them.

Strikes among the men on the work were frequent and these

were also usually settled by the police. Undoubtedly the force was an important factor in making possible the rapid advance and completion of the Canadian Pacific Railway.

In 1883 occurred another notable event — the Old Man's River had nearly completed the destruction of Macleod village and was undermining the fort itself. A new fort was therefore built on the bench land in 1884 and the original abandoned. The need for a stockade was ended. The new fort was an open square, comfortable both for men and horses, in great contrast to the old cottonwood stockade built in 1874 with its mud floors and roof. It utterly disappeared in 1884 and the Old Man's River today rolls over the site of the first fort built by the North-West Mounted Police in the present province of Alberta.

The old nine-pound guns brought across the plains in 1874 at much cost in toil and horseflesh were also moved for the first time since placed in the old fort 10 years before. While the fort was being built, construction was begun on a number of buildings a little to the east and the new town of Macleod came into being. There was a great contrast between the old mud-roofed log buildings of the first town and the neat lumber structures of the new.

Macleod had boasted a newspaper, the *Macleod Gazette,* founded and edited by a former police constable, C. E. D. Wood, in 1882. This was the second newspaper published in Alberta, the *Edmonton Bulletin,* owned and edited by Frank Oliver, being the first. It was established in the previous year. The *Calgary Herald* commenced publication in 1883.

It might be said that the official history of Alberta commenced in 1882 when Rupert's Land was organized into four provincial districts: Alberta, Saskatchewan, Assiniboia, and Athabasca. In 1875 a separate legislative body under a Lieutenant-Governor was given the Territories. Provision also was made for elected representatives in the North-West Council. When any district contained a white population of 1,000, an election might be held and a parliamentary representative sent to the Council. In 1876 the Honorable David Laird was appointed Lieutenant-Governor of the Territories and the first session of the North-West Council was held at Swan River on March 8, 1877.

In 1880, to quote from an early history of the future Alberta capital, the "town of Edmonton consisted of only five white families and a number of half-breeds, but people were beginning to be attracted there and soon what was known as claim-jumping began to worry the few original inhabitants. As the country was unsurveyed, the settlers had no actual rights in the land and the newcomers attempted to squat and build themselves shacks wherever they fancied. This led to the election of a vigilance committee, with Mr. Matthew McCauley, a sturdy

Sergeant Wilde, sitting, and a Constable removed the tents that Chiefs Piapot and Long Man had erected across the railway right-of-way. In an unrelated incident, Wilde was later murdered by an Indian named Charcoal.

The Indians could only watch as the railway changed forever the land whose buffalo had provided food, clothing and shelter for centuries.

pioneer, as its captain. Whenever a newcomer attempted to squat on land already claimed, he was promptly warned, and if he still persisted, the committee proceeded to throw his shack over the river bank into what was called the Vigilantes' Depository. This action was highly exciting at times but proved effective."

In 1883 the Canadian Pacific reached Calgary and all freight was teamed from there to Edmonton. There was also a weekly stagecoach. The passenger rate for a quick journey — express — was $100.

In 1883, according to Dr. George Roy, an old-timer in Edmonton, there were between 35 and 40 houses. In all the region between Calgary and Edmonton, except around Red Deer River crossing, there was no white settlement. In 1891 the Canadian Pacific put on a regular service over their new Calgary and Edmonton branch and while the trip took two days, it was a vast improvement over the ox-trail. Shipments of grain and cattle went over the new road, the first real outlet for the agricultural resources of the north country. The days of the Hudson's Bay Company's trading monopoly were over. As settlement for their claims they received a cash payment of $1.5 million and one-twentieth of the land south of the North and main Saskatchewan Rivers.

During the years 1882-83, the liquor business flourished, more particularly in Calgary. The police found it most difficult to secure sufficient evidence for conviction, owing principally to the number of permits granted. Liquor was now seldom traded to the Indians. It was more profitable to dispose of it to white men in the towns springing up along the line of the Canadian Pacific Railway.

The site of the present city of Lethbridge had until 1884 gone under the name of Coal Banks. It was owned by the North-West Coal and Navigation Company. This company, during the building of the Canadian Pacific, had done a large coal business with that railway, shipping coal in barges down the river to Medicine Hat. In 1885 the branch from Lethbridge to Dunmore on the main line of the Canadian Pacific Railway near Medicine Hat was finished, and with the railroad came the settlers.

In the following year Lethbridge had a population of 1,000 and buildings went up in all directions. When the town site was surveyed and laid out in 1884 the question of naming it arose. Coal Banks was discarded and Government was petitioned to change the name to Coleridge. This was thought inexpedient as there was already a town of that name in Ontario. Then the coal company, really the founder of the town, offered to name it after its president, William Lethbridge, of London, England.

Since there was no objection, Lethbridge it became.

I have often thought it a pity that more of the Indian names for prominent towns were not retained. Many of these were most appropriate and in most cases far more musical than the translations into English, such as Moose Jaw, Medicine Hat and others.

The duties of the police during 1883-84 were extremely heavy. The field of their operations had been greatly extended. All over the country settlers were entering in large numbers, making crime much more prevalent. During 1884, five murders were recorded — two by Indians, two by white men, and one by a negro.

The murder by the negro was a particularly cold-blooded one. Late one night it was reported to Superintendent Steele, commanding at Calgary, that a man named Adams had committed suicide in the town. But when Inspector Dowling and Dr. Kennedy examined the body they decided that it was a case of murder, not suicide.

A negro named Williams had been seen in conversation with Adams earlier in the evening. He was trailed by Sergeant-Major Lake through the freshly fallen snow to the yard behind the Cochrane Ranch Company's butcher shop where, hidden under the corner of a hayrack, a leather glove stuffed with bills was picked up. A few minutes later he was arrested and the mate to the glove and a blood-stained razor were found in his shack. Stains on his clothing he explained as made by some beef he had been carrying, but the evidence against him was too direct. He ultimately confessed and became the first man to be hanged in Calgary.

Calgary in 1883. By then the community was growing rapidly, its population trebling from some 7,000 in 1881 to over 21,000 by 1884.

CHAPTER FOURTEEN

Indians in a Changing West

From self rule and the freedom of the plains, the Indians have to adapt to being governed by whites and confined to reserves.

Since 1882 I had been in charge as Indian Agent of the Indians, numbering close to 7,000 in Treaty Number Seven and of the two Indian supply farms. Monthly visits to the various reserves, in most cases long distances apart, with my duties in the office at Macleod, kept myself and clerk fully occupied. A farm instructor and ration issuer for each reserve, with my driver and three men employed on the industrial farm, completed my staff. The Indians on all reservations in the treaty did well with their crops in 1883. The Blackfeet, Bloods, and Piegans turned in 1,100 sacks of potatoes to be stored for their use in the agency root houses. The Piegans did particularly well, using their own horses and having as many as 10 ploughs going at one time. At least 600 acres were turned over in the agency during the year, none of it by contract. The Indians, besides the ploughing, did all fencing, building, etc.

The Bloods were more settled and contented than ever before. Few left their homes to cross the Line on horse stealing expeditions, although on one occasion when I was in camp a large band of stolen horses was brought in. I took possession of the animals, which were returned to the owners a few days later. The following details are taken from my report to the Superintendent-General of Indian Affairs for 1883:

"The Stony Indians' cattle are doing as well as can be expected. A few have mixed with the Cochrane Ranch Company herds, but as this company are moving their cattle south, no further trouble from this source will occur. I have made a contract to have all the lumber cut by the Stonies rafted down the Bow River to the Blackfoot Crossing, to be used by those

Head of the Mountain Detachment in 1886. By horseback and buggy police regularly visited settlers on the prairie, getting each to sign a patrol sheet. The

Indians as roofing and flooring for the buildings they are putting up. The timber on their reserve will last the Stonies for years if carefully used and they might be allowed to sell small quantities of the lumber which they make by whip-sawing. They are good hunters and trappers and I think before long they will be able to support and look after themselves. The Sarcees have about one hundred and seventy-five acres under cultivation, but have not been as quiet as I should have wished. A few of the worst characters have caused trouble during the summer, but have been arrested and punished."

By the fall of 1883 instances of our Indians crossing to United States territory on horse stealing expeditions had largely ceased, although there were still many instances of Indians and white men from Montana making raids on this side. The system of granting permits to Indians to leave their reserve was found unworkable. An Indian wishing to go south on an unlawful expedition would be the last to ask for a permit since he could slip away unnoticed whenever so inclined. Also in making this provision the Government lost sight of the fact that one clause of the Treaty of 1877 distinctly stated that Indians had the right to travel in any part of the country, subject to the laws thereof. This clause the Indians never forgot. When they were required to obtain permits it was always brought up

miles they drove or rode were astonishing. For instance, one year Constable Armour drove over 3,000 miles — a distance considered no more than average.

and was impossible to overlook.

Previous to 1882 all money for the Indian annuity payments came from Fort Benton through the firm of I. G. Baker & Company at Fort Macleod and was in bills of American currency. Thereafter, until banks were established at Calgary and other growing towns, the money came direct to the Indian Agent from Ottawa, though in most inconvenient form.

Uncut sheets of Canadian $1 bills were delivered in a box the size of a small tea-chest. In Treaty Number Seven, of which as Agent I was in charge, the payments were around $40,000. The task of reducing these sheets of 18 units to bundles containing 100 bills may thus be realized. It was thought that making all payments in $1 bills would lessen the likelihood of the Indians being cheated. They would thus become more quickly acquainted with their value than if paid in bills of different denominations. This theory was probably true, but it entailed much extra work and anxiety on the part of the Indian Agent making the payments.

Before the coming of the railroads, the Agents travelled in light wagons from reserve to reserve. In some cases they travelled long distances over country without trails where guides were necessary and with large amounts of money, camping at night in all weathers and usually accompanied only by a single

Mounted policeman or the driver. That not one case of robbery or loss of this money ever occurred shows, perhaps better than anything else, the respect for the law which had been established through the North-West Mounted Police.

Across the Boundary Line conditions were vastly different. Hardly a month passed that did not bring its tale of stage robbery, mine hold-up, or murder. Even army paymasters were stopped and the money taken. Although many responsible for these crimes were hanged or shot, crime was still prevalent. Maintenance of law and order suffered greatly in comparison with that obtained in the Canadian North-West.

With the disappearance of the buffalo and their replacement by large herds of stock, cattle killing, and more particularly horse stealing, became prevalent. Indians, either Canadian or American, were not the only culprits. Lawless white men from the American side crossed the Line to steal in Canada because it was safer. If caught in Montana they received little sympathy from the Vigilance Committee and were likely to end their careers hanging from the handiest tree.

In Canada, on the other hand, in the event of capture they were always assured of a fair trial and, at the worst, imprisonment. They were seldom caught, as it was easy for them to cross into Montana where they found a ready market for the stolen stock. No assistance to punish these thieves or recover the stolen stock could be secured from the American authorities. There was no extradition treaty between Canada and the United States for several years after the settlement of the North-West Territories.

The liquor traffic, which in the first five years after the arrival of the Mounted Police had been nearly stamped out, again began to grow into serious proportions. Its elimination was almost as disagreeable a duty as any the police had to perform. By the prohibitionists of the community they were condemned as being too lax, while the non-temperance partisans found them too severe. Information against these lawbreakers was almost impossible to obtain. No settler, however much he was against the sale of liquor, would turn informer, and none of the traders themselves would do so for the half of the fine to be derived by giving such information.

The profit was immense, as much as $100 being realized at times from the sale of a five-gallon keg. It was necessary that police detachments be stationed near the Boundary Line, as most of the liquor came from Montana. The trains on the Canadian Pacific had also to be watched, as liquor was also smuggled over the rails. The mails on that road from Moose Jaw westward were also under charge of members of the force. These men were sworn in as Special Constables of the postal authorities and carried out their duties greatly to the satisfaction of that department. It will therefore be seen how varied had become the duties of the force.

In 1883-84 many new police posts were established at points along the railroad and in the vicinity of the Indian reservations, and patrols were constantly on the move. A new town blossomed at Macleod, Lethbridge was on the map, and Edmonton, Regina, Battleford, and Prince Albert were growing rapidly and innumerable villages were springing up along the line of railroad.

Calgary, first located east of the Elbow River, had by 1883 become a thriving town. Land originally taken by myself as a homestead but which had passed to the ownership of Major John Stewart was first selected by the Canadian Pacific Railway as their town site. However, the figure placed upon it was too high to suit the railway authorities. They went across the Elbow to the west side and built a permanent station and freight shed with the result that the whole town followed.

Many cattle ranches were also launched during these years in the Calgary district. Fred Stimson, manager of the Bar U, sent Tom Lynch to Lost River, Idaho, for cattle to stock his range. He also imported 21 head of thoroughbred bulls. Lynch purchased a herd of 3,000, leaving Lost River in May and arriving at High River in September. He brought with him a colored man named John Ware who became a noted character among the High River cowboys. "Nigger John" was a first-rate rough rider, champion roper, and all-round cattleman. He remained with the Bar U outfit for many years, finally going into ranching for himself. He was accidentally killed on the range in 1904.

One of the greatest menaces to stockmen was timber wolves. In the buffalo days the large timber wolf followed the buffalo herds in packs and on the disappearance of the buffalo took to the hills. When cattle came in, they preyed on them, causing great loss. A full-grown wolf was calculated to do $1,000 worth of damage yearly. Young stock suffered most, though older stock was also killed. Colts were easy victims as the mares would run and the youngsters became separated from their mothers, when they were soon pulled down. Calves were not so readily killed. The cattle would bunch up and present a formidable front of sharp horns to the enemy. Stock of all ages was found all over the range badly mutilated and usually hamstrung so that they would eventually die or have to be killed.

Bounties were offered, both by the Stock Association and the Government, of $5 and $10 for a wolf scalp. Hounds of all breeds — wolfhounds, boarhounds, greyhounds and other dogs — were used to hunt the pests. They were dug out of dens and the pups killed. But as long as cattle in great numbers ranged southern

Alberta, the large grey wolf continued to take toll of the herds.

As already mentioned, the Cochrane Ranch Company was first located near Ghost River, west of Calgary, but owing to heavy losses moved to a new lease on the Belly River south of Macleod. This company purchased a second herd of some 6,000 head in Montana and added them to the herd already on their range. These cattle were also in poor condition. At the beginning of the unusually severe winter of 1882-83, there were at least 12,000 cattle on the Cochrane ranch west of Calgary. In the spring a scant 4,000 remained. Dead bodies were heaped in every coulee. Some of the long ravines were so filled with carcasses that a man would go from top to bottom throughout the entire length and never step off a dead body. Despite these set-backs, by the close of 1884 there were at least 40,000 range animals in what is today southern Alberta.

About this time there was excitement in the Rocky Mountains near today's Banff. A reputed find of silver resulted in the birth of a community called Silver City. But the excitement quickly died. It was discovered that the specimens of rich silver ore which Joe Healy, one of the original owners of Whoop-up, and a man named Clinker Scott had claimed was yielded by their claims near Castle Mountain, had really been imported from Montana. The boom collapsed and Silver City became only a memory.

The Indians, meanwhile, were beginning to reconcile themselves to the disappearance of the buffalo, and to realize their only salvation lay in trying to raise crops and stock. It was not to be expected, however, that they would be immediately successful or that they would not for many years be more or less dependent upon the Government for help and support. They had been a free and happy race, knowing no law or restraint but their own will or the tribal rule. Now they were like people suddenly shut off from light, having blindly to grope their way towards a new and unknown condition of which they had no conception. They were wards of the Government in every sense, not only of duty but by right. Only sympathetic and intelligent handling would prevent their sharing the fate of other primitive peoples.

The white settler coming into the country to raise cattle or farm cared little what became of the poor Indian. If a cow was killed or a horse stolen, the Indians were to blame. Their land was looked upon with covetous eyes and they were regarded as a nuisance and expense. The right of the native red man was not for a moment considered or acknowledged, though more from ignorance than actual hard-heartedness. He was an inferior being to the lordly white man and doomed to pass before advancing civilization.

CHAPTER FIFTEEN

The North-West Rebellion

Incompetent Civil Servants and Politicians who ignored the Policemen's warnings trigger an unnecessary war.

The Deputy Superintendent-General of Indian Affairs, visiting the West in 1884, made a hurried trip to Fort Macleod. Although pressed by me to visit some of the Indian reservations, he declined to do so and after a few days returned to Ottawa. He was backward even in meeting the Indian chiefs who came to Macleod to see him. This was unfortunate, as he might by personal observation during his stay have gained some knowledge of the conditions prevailing in Treaty Number Seven. I later received from him an official letter, from which I take the following quotation:

"I have to inform you that the Superintendent-General is of the opinion that there exists no necessity for employing a clerk in your office; consequently you will, after giving him a month's warning, discharge him, as it is considered that you ought to be capable of performing all the office work in your agency, as well as supervising the issue of rations supplied from the store. The storekeeper should therefore be dismissed and you are consequently required to act as storekeeper and to restrict yourself to one visit each month to each of the reserves within your district and on making your visits you are to lock your office and storehouses and take the interpreter with you to act as servant and interpreter. The Superintendent-General is of the opinion that no assistant instructors are necessary and that the employment of officials has a bad effect. The instructors ought to be able to supervise all the Indians in their district."

My answer to this epistle was to promptly forward my resignation to Ottawa. My letter reads:

"I have the honour to inform you ... that I have notified my clerk and also the storekeeper of the instructions contained therein. This is most hard on the clerk, who has only just arrived after a long journey. I beg to inform you that I cannot undertake to do this work and I therefore think it best to notify you of the same, as I have always, and shall always, do my work thoroughly and I do not see my way to do so in this instance. The work of a clerk in my office takes all his time from one month's end to the other and I cannot do this and look after the Treaty. I also cannot see my way to cut down the Indian rations as ordered, as to do so would without doubt bring on trouble. My work has been difficult since I came here but am glad to say that everything in the Treaty is in perfect order and I do not wish while I am here to see it upset. I therefore beg that I be allowed to resign my position as agent of this Treaty as soon as convenient to the Detachment. I have applied for leave from the First of March, and if my place is filled before that time I shall be glad while I am here to assist the new agent all in my power."

The Commissioner of the Mounted Police and the different Indian agents also received an order cancelling issuance of permits to Indians to leave their reservations, a step recommended by the same Deputy Superintendent-General of Indian Affairs. The Commissioner's comment on this order, when reporting to the Premier, was:

"This shows a total want of knowledge on his (the Deputy Superintendent-General's) part of the treaties made with the western Indians, in which it was distinctly stipulated that they might travel anywhere through the country, subject to the law of the land, and I wish to point out that the introduction of such a system would be tantamount to a breach of confidence with the Indians generally, inasmuch as from the outset the Indians have been led to believe that compulsory residence on reservations would not be required of them and that they would be permitted to travel about for legitimate hunting and trading purposes. This concession largely contributed to the satisfactory conclusion of the treaty with the Blackfeet."

Upon quitting my position on receipt of the cutback orders, Treaty Number Seven was divided into three separate agencies. Each had an Agent at the same salary as that I received while in charge of the whole and aided by a clerk, farm instructor, assistant, and other subordinates. The short-sightedness and absurdity of the order is therefore apparent and evidence of a lamentable ignorance of Western Indian reservations and conditions. Worse, after my resignation orders were sent to cut down the rations. This reduction in food was, at least in some measure, no doubt a contributing cause of the outbreak among the Indians along the Saskatchewan in the following year.

Towards the close of 1884 the Indians throughout the North-West were showing unmistakable symptoms of restlessness. This situation caused much anxiety to both police and Indian Department officials in close touch with them and with the half-breeds (Metis), and aware of their real and fancied grievances. Representations made to Ottawa as to the danger of an outbreak were ignored or regarded as visionary. But the clash when it came in the spring of 1885 was no surprise to those familiar with the situation in the North-West.

Among other incidents which portended trouble may be mentioned the following: Sergeant Fury, with a constable and the interpreter, arrested at the Blackfoot Crossing a Blackfoot named Whitecap for horse stealing. They were surrounded by a mob of Indians indignant over the reduction of their rations, who threatened to release the prisoner by force. Fury was obliged to leave without the Indian. But upon his reporting, Superintendent Steele left at once with 30 men for the Crossing to arrest the leaders in the obstruction of the previous day. In the meantime the latter, having become worried over the outcome, had gone by a different route into Calgary. Here they were arrested and, after a reprimand from the judge, released.

At Crooked Lakes, near Broadview, a large camp of Crees had gathered to hold a medicine dance. They danced for a week when, their militant ardour having been sufficiently aroused, a large party broke into the agency storehouse and helped themselves to a quantity of provisions. A Mounted Police detail under Superintendent Deane was dispatched to the reserve but was unable to effect any arrests. Headquarters was wired for reinforcements which arrived next day under Superintendent W. M. Herchmer. The augmented force moved towards the Indian camp but were halted by a large party of armed and excited warriors. A parley ensured and surrender of the ringleaders of the raid was demanded. They refused and a determined show of resistance was offered, a house nearby bristling with the muzzles of levelled rifles.

Since most of the police were covered at short distance, it would have been foolhardy under the circumstances to advance. Following a second long parley, the police drew off and took up their quarters in another adjacent house. Two days more of palaver resulted in the surrender of four of the Indians, one the chief, Yellow Calf. The latter, however, having aided the police in attaining their purpose, was later released. The other three were tried and discharged by Judge Richardson at Regina. It was probably the most satisfactory conclusion, as the Commissioner stated in his report, to a troublesome affair.

Others among the southern Crees were becoming very trou-

North-West Mounted Police at Fort Carlton in 1884. A few months later, with citizen volunteers from Prince Albert, they engaged the Metis and Indians in the disastrous first battle of the North-West, or Riel, Rebellion. Of the 99 police and volunteers, 21 were wounded or killed. A few days later when the Fort was being evacuated, it partly burned down, then was destroyed by the Indians and Metis. Today, much of it has been restored and is open to the public.

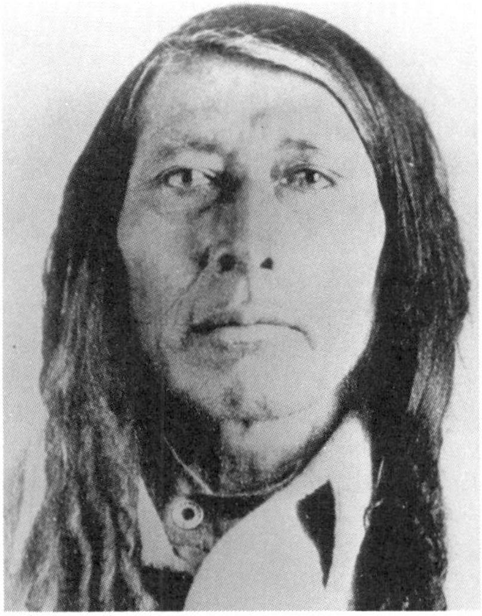

Cree Chief Poundmaker, above, was among the instigators of the Rebellion. Gabriel Dumont, at top right, was the brilliant Metis leader. Had Riel listened to him, they would have killed or captured all of the policemen. During the battle Dumont was seriously wounded and his brother killed.

Sheltered in the log building below, Metis sharpshooters poured deadly fire into the Prince Albert Volunteers, killing nine.

blesome, many leaving their reserves and going north. A man named Pollock was shot at Maple Creek, presumably by Indians. Sergeant Patterson followed the trail 100 miles to the boundary-line without overhauling them. A band of horses stolen at the same time in the same vicinity was not recovered.

There was trouble, also, of a serious character among the Crees near Battleford. On Poundmaker's reserve, farm instructor Craig was assaulted by an Indian and his band refused to give the offender up. Superintendent Crozier went with 25 men to arrest him. The Indians were holding a sun dance and Superintendent Crozier decided to defer action until its conclusion. Meanwhile, he sent for reinforcements to Battleford and moved the provisions from the Government storehouse some three miles to an old building which his men converted into a temporary fort. As the police passed the camp on the way to this building the Indians staged a sham attack, their bullets whistling unpleasantly close to the heads of the police.

The building having been put into as good a state for defence as possible and the reinforcements having arrived, upon the conclusion of the sun dance negotiations were opened. But the Indians persisted in their refusal to surrender the culprit. In the end he was taken from them by force, but amid scenes of confusion and excitement that escaped almost by a miracle culminating in a bloody debacle. Prominent in this affair were Poundmaker, Big Bear, Lucky Man, and other old chiefs who took a leading part in the Riel Rebellion of the following year. Superintendent Crozier gave the greatest praise to the coolness and steadiness of the detachment under his command.

Twenty-five horses disappeared this fall from the vicinity of Maple Creek, a half-breed who was herding them being found dead. All but three were recovered later from the Bloods and Piegans near Macleod, but the murderer was never identified. Two of the thieves were subsequently arrested and sent to the penitentiary for two years.

These conditions continued throughout the winter and into the spring of 1885, gradually growing worse. The half-breeds and Crees along the Saskatchewan became constantly bolder and more defiant. In March matters culminated in open rebellion, an outcome foreseen as early as June of the previous year. The half-breeds in that summer had invited Louis Riel from Montana to champion their cause, as he had done in the previous rebellion of 1869. Throughout the fall and winter of 1884, reports reached the police of frequent meetings of the half-breeds, at which they listened to inflammatory speeches made by Riel.

The half-breed population of the North-West was settled

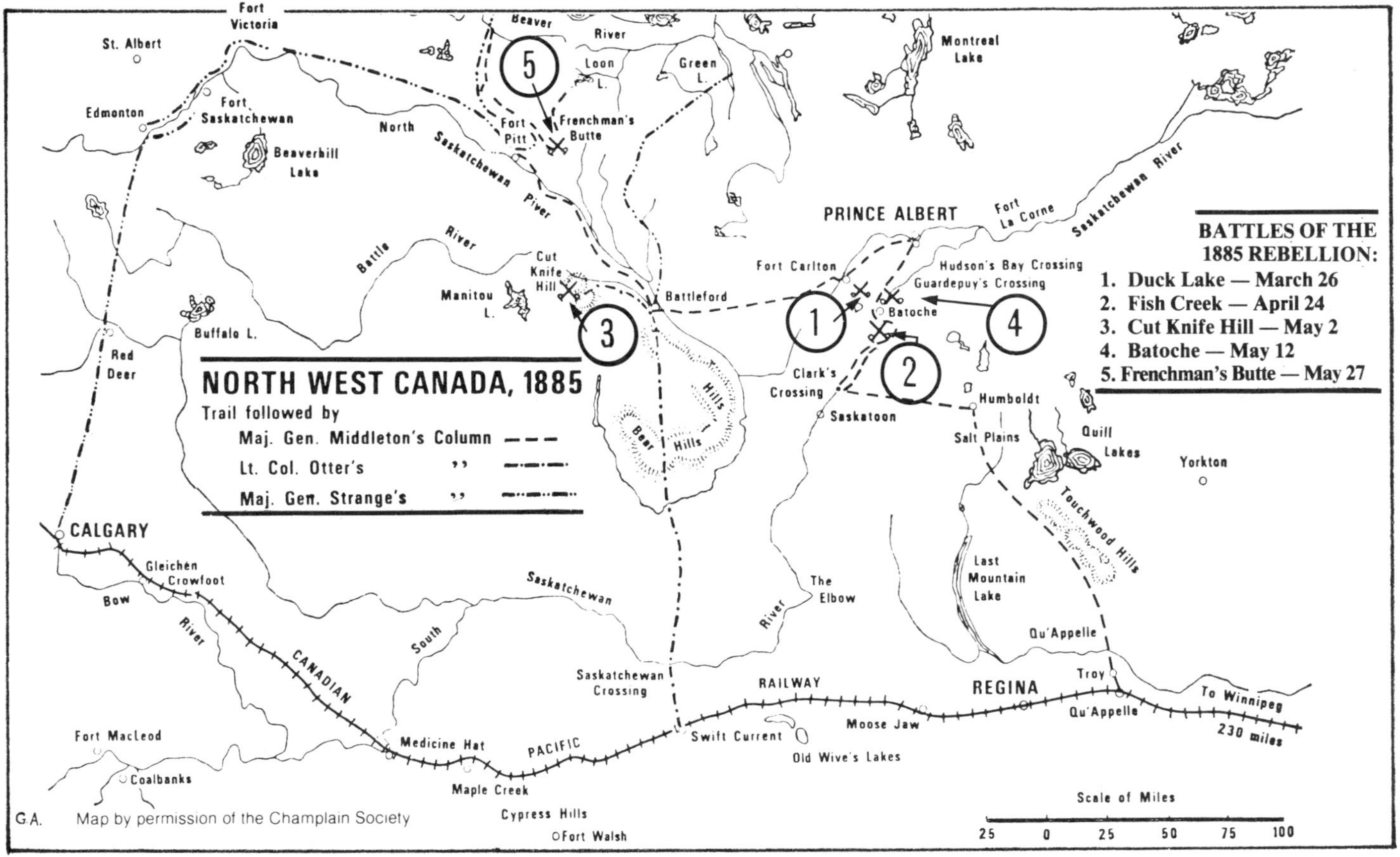

The North-West Territories in 1885 showing the five main encounters during the Riel Rebellion and routes followed by the three columns of mounted police and militia.

mainly along the North and South Saskatchewan Rivers in the vicinity of Fort Carlton, Prince Albert, Duck Lake, and Battleford. Farming was little to their taste, for they were by upbringing and instinct essentially hunters, trappers, and nomads. Many had followed the buffalo into Montana. On the disappearance of the shaggy herds in that country they returned, with few exceptions, to the Saskatchewan to find their means of livelihood seriously curtailed. In the old days, the half-breed trapper and voyageur had thrived under the fur companies, but with the arrival of railroads and settlers had come an end to those modes of existence.

Among their grievances was the system of land survey in square blocks of townships and sections. Previously the land had been laid out in narrow lots, two miles long and fronting the rivers, permitting close communal association. Under the new plan they were afraid of losing a portion of their holdings and turned to Riel as the man to head the popular agitation and secure redress of their real or fancied wrongs.

Riel was a man of weak personality. Indian, French, Irish, and Scandinavian blood ran in his veins. He was vain, inordinately susceptible to flattery, and he welcomed any opportunity for theatrical display. His first meetings were held at Prince Albert and Duck Lake. The Mounted Police kept close watch on events in the north during the winter of 1884.

Superintendent Gagnon reported in December that the half-breeds of St. Laurent and Batoche had held a public meeting to adopt a petition to be forwarded to Ottawa. This petition was called the Bill of Rights. Its demands were: (1) Subdivision of the North-West Territories into provinces; (2) The extension to all half-breeds of land grants of 240 acres and advantages enjoyed by the Manitoba half-breeds; (3) The issue of patents to all colonists then in possession; (4) The sale of 500,000 acres of Dominion lands, the proceeds of which were to be expended on building schools, hospitals, and similar institutions in the half-breed settlements and in equipping the poorer classes with seed grain and agricultural implements; (5) The reservation of 100 townships of swamp lands to be distributed among the children of half-breeds during the next 120 years; (6) Money grants for certain religious institutions and better provision for the Indians.

Riel made the Indians believe that their title to the lands in the North-West had never been properly extinguished. In addition, he held out many promises of future rewards to the chiefs should they join him.

No attention was paid to the petition. Indeed, it was ignored and the Government attached no importance to the rumours that discontent was very widespread throughout the

North-West. If these claims had been examined, it would have been found that there certainly was some ground for the half-breeds' grievances, more particularly in the matter of security in the holding of their farms. Had timely consideration been given to their claims and steps been taken to deal with them, it is possible that no outbreak would have occurred.

The half-breeds, despite their many human weaknesses, were found by the police to be as a whole a law-abiding and loyal people so long as they were fairly dealt with. That when considerately treated they could be firm friends was shown when Sitting Bull invited them to join in a war of extermination against the white man. Their reply was that they would fight for the whites and not against them. In 1885 many of them were openly hostile to Riel. In fact, men such as Peter Hourie, Peter Erasmus, and McKay family rendered invaluable service as guides, scouts, and interpreters to the Government forces engaged in military operations during that year.

On March 10 Superintendent Gagnon wired the Commissioner that the half-breeds were becoming increasingly active and that they proposed to prevent supplies going in after the sixteenth. A few days later Superintendent Crozier asked that a nine-pound gun and 25 men be sent to Battleford. He also telegraphed: "Half-breed rebellion liable to break out any moment. If half-breeds rise, Indians will join them."

Colonel Irvine moved promptly. On March 18 he left Regina with all his available force — four officers, 86 non-commissioned officers and men and 66 horses. At the Salt Plain he learned from Crozier that some Indians had already joined and that others were likely at any hour to join the rebels. Their numbers were estimated as between 200 and 400. At Humboldt further word reached him that some 400 half-breeds had assembled at Batoche to prevent him joining Crozier. On the twenty-third the rebels broke camp and soon afterwards the Colonel was notified that the mail station at Hoodoo had been sacked. Arriving there, he found that in addition to removing all provisions and grain, the raiders had captured the stage-driver with his horses.

The Commissioner arrived at Prince Albert on the twenty-fourth, avoiding the half-breeds waiting to intercept him at Batoche by turning off and taking a northeasterly direction towards Agnew's Crossing of the South Saskatchewan, to the intense chagrin of Riel's militant adherents. At Prince Albert, Colonel Irvine remained two days to rest the horses after their march of 290 miles. Meanwhile, he enrolled a body of volunteers to protect the town, and then proceeded to Carlton. When within a few miles from that place, word came from Superin-

Sam Steele was among the first to enlist in the NWMP, his bravery and devotion to duty making him a legend. He is shown in his early 50s. By then he had served over 20 years on the prairie, kept peace and order during construction of the CPR, quelled a potential Indian uprising in B.C., been in command of B.C.-Yukon during the Klondike Stampede and served with distinction in the Boer War.

Below: Steele's Scouts during the Riel Rebellion. With Steele, these men pursued and captured Big Bear. Although several of them were wounded or killed during the Rebellion, the Mounties were initially denied a medal issued to those who helped quell the uprising.

tendent Gagnon that Crozier had met the half-breeds near Duck Lake in a hot engagement. He had been obliged to retreat after severe losses in killed and wounded.

From details of the Duck Lake fight in Superintendent Crozier's report, it is learned that he had on the morning of the twenty-sixth dispatched Sergeant Stewart and 17 men, with Joseph McKay of Prince Albert as guide, to bring in some police provisions and ammunition stored with a trader named Hilliard Mitchell at Duck Lake.

They were met near that place by a large party of armed half-breeds who insolently demanded their surrender and threatened to fire upon them. The police ignored this demand. Then McKay informed the rebels that the firing, should it commence, would not all be on one side. Stewart and his men held the insurgents off and retired towards Carlton, sending a man ahead to notify the commanding officer. Superintendent Crozier left Carlton immediately with all the men he could muster, numbering, with the Prince Albert Volunteers, 100 and with a nine-pound gun. He met and was joined by Stewart and his detail and continued towards Duck Lake to secure the stores they had been prevented from obtaining.

At the point where Stewart had encountered them, he found his further progress blocked by the rebels. In the meantime, they had been strongly reinforced and selected their position with much strategic skill. Superintendent Crozier posted his men to the best advantage, but they were in a hopeless minority. The sleighs were their only cover and, the snow being deep, rapid movement was impossible. After a half hour the police were forced to retreat. Nine of the Prince Albert Volunteers were killed and five badly wounded, while three police were killed and six wounded.

Superintendent Crozier himself behaved on this occasion with the greatest gallantry, coolly pacing back and forth in front of his men, who were either lying down or under shelter behind the sleighs, and encouraging them by his voice and example. I learned from Peter Hourie that Gabriel Dumont, commander of the half-breeds, had given an order that Major Crozier was not to be fired upon while continually in plain view in front of the line. This order the half-breed leader explained as having been prompted by the admiration which the cool courage displayed by the officer had excited in him.

With the Duck Lake fight, the half-breeds and Indians threw down the gauntlet to the Government and went into open hostility. On Superintendent Crozier's return to Carlton, Commissioner Colonel Irvine, who meanwhile had arrived with 80 men from Prince Albert, decided to abandon Carlton and fall back to

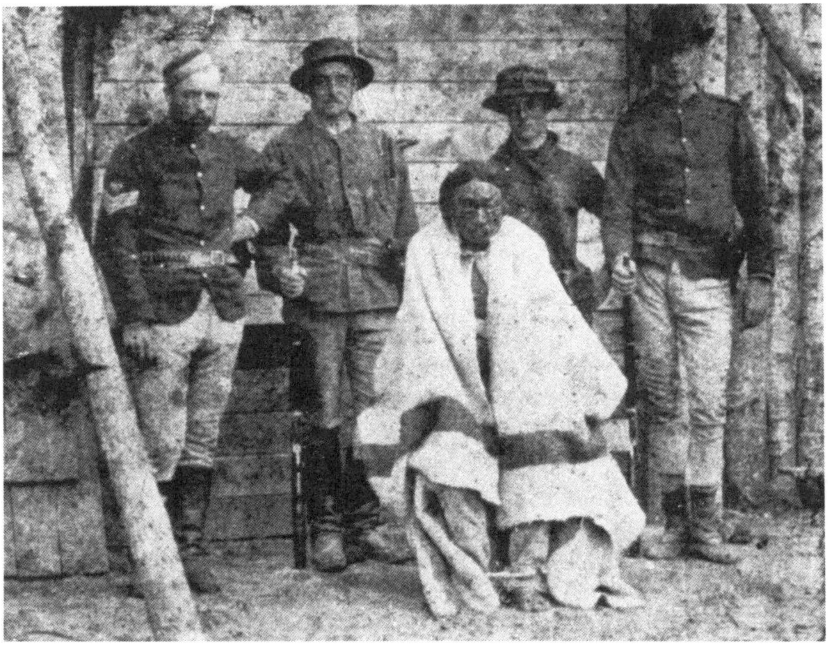

Big Bear after capture by Steele's Scouts. On his left is Sergeant Colin Colebrook who in 1895 was murdered by an Indian, Almighty Voice. The murder began a chain of violent acts that resulted in two more policemen and an ex-policeman being killed, as well as Almighty Voice and two companions.

Prince Albert to protect that town, in which all the loyal settlers in the district had taken refuge. Carlton was consequently abandoned on 28th March. At the moment of departure of the force, this landmark of historic associations in Hudson's Bay Company annals accidentally caught fire and burned to the ground.

Prince Albert, which was in daily expectation of an attack by the rebels, welcomed with great relief the return of Colonel Irvine and his command. The defences of the town were immediately strengthened. The days that followed were anxious ones, both for police and volunteers. The safety of some 2,000 people, among them many women and children, was in their keeping. The defenders numbered 225 Mounted Police and 300 volunteers.

The Government at Ottawa was now fully awake to the gravity of the situation and troops under Major-General Sir Fred Middleton, Commander-in-Chief of the Canadian Militia, were rushed from the East to the scene of the outbreak. In April troops began to arrive and Qu'Appelle became the base of operations. Three columns were dispatched, one under General T. B. Strange to operate against Big Bear in the territory east of

Edmonton, another under Colonel W. D. Otter to relieve beleaguered Battleford, and the third commanded by General Middleton to strike at the heart of the rebellion at Batoche and relieve Prince Albert. The total of these forces, with the artillery, guides, and scouts, numbered over 4,000 men.

The history of the campaign of 1885 has been written many times. General Strange, an old artillery officer, marched north from Calgary with the Alberta Field Force to Edmonton, thence east along the north bank of the Saskatchewan to attack Big Bear whose cut-throat band of plains Crees had slaughtered nine defenceless whites at Frog Lake and taken a number of prisoners.

At Edmonton, where Superintendent A. H. Griesbach was in command of the Mounted Police, no serious outrages had occurred. However, the Indians of Bob Tail's and Ermine Skin's bands had plundered the Hudson's Bay stores at Battle River and the settlers round Beaver Lake, who fled to Fort Saskatchewan for protection. Depredations were also committed at Lac la Biche. On the approach of General Strange's force the chiefs of these bands surrendered and there was no further trouble in that district, the settlers returning to their homes. General Strange defeated the Indians under Big Bear at Frenchman's Butte and released the prisoners held by him. Big Bear escaped after that engagement, but on learning that Riel had been routed and the rebel chief himself captured by General Middleton on May 11 at Batoche, the old Cree leader gave himself up to the Mounted Police at Carlton, 200 miles away from the scene of the Frenchman's Butte engagement.

Poundmaker and other chiefs surrendered to General Middleton at Battleford. With the defeat and capture of all the leaders, the rebellion of 1885 came to an end. Louis Riel was hanged at Regina. Eight Indians, convicted of murders at Frog Lake and Battleford, were hanged in November at the latter place, a fitting punishment for their crimes.

Chief Big Bear was sentenced to three years in Stony Mountain Penitentiary but was released at the end of 14 months. It was proven at his trial that while he was no doubt in sympathy — as was natural — with his relatives, the half-breeds, he had personally had no part in the massacre at Frog Lake. On the contrary, he had tried to prevent it. He died shortly after his release on Little Pine's reserve near Battleford.

Poundmaker received a prison sentence of two years, but, like Big Bear, he did not long survive his liberation. He died while on a visit to Chief Crowfoot of the Blackfoot in 1888 at Blackfoot Crossing.

CHAPTER SIXTEEN

Keeping Peace During the Rebellion

The police persuade the Blackfoot and other tribes not to join Riel, then are again betrayed by the politicians.

In southern Alberta the Indians had remained quiet during the winter. In the spring, however, when their rations were much reduced and unsettling rumours reached them regarding prospective trouble in the north, they became dissatisfied and restless.

Then came the news of the Duck Lake fight. I was called up at my ranch about three miles from Macleod late one night in March 1885, and told that Superintendent John Cotton, commanding the Mounted Police in the district, wished to see me at the fort. I went over at once — to find the barracks in a considerable state of excitement. Word had just been received of the outbreak of the rebellion in the north.

The Superintendent was most anxious for me to again take charge of the Indians in Treaty Number Seven, which, as I have mentioned, since my quitting the previous year had been divided into three agencies under three separate agents. He informed me that matters were not going well with the different bands; that the agents were unable to control them. He feared also that these Indians might take advantage of the trouble in the north to start killing cattle and to commit other depredations, more particularly since their rations having been reduced they were not given sufficient food.

I declined to consider the proposal unless with the understanding that I should have full control and that there would be no interference from officials in Ottawa such as had previously occurred. He said he would at once wire the Lieutenant-Governor my conditions and asked me to accompany him to the Blood reservation next day. He wished me to talk to the chiefs, who he thought would listen to me. We left in the morning and on our arrival were told by the Agent, Mr. Pocklington, that the Indians would not listen to him and were bent on mischief.

I sent word to all chiefs in the camp to come to the agency for a council. In a short time they assembled to the number of about 30. I told them of the outbreak of the Crees and advised them to remain quietly on their reserves. Complaints were many, the chief that they had not enough to eat.

The Crees, they said, were their long-time enemies and they would not join them as they had been asked to do. They would, however, if allowed go on the warpath against them. The Agent was blamed for the decrease in rations and they had grievances against other white men on the reserve. Superintendent Cotton at the end asked me to tell them that anything I promised would be carried out.

Before the council closed a messenger arrived from Macleod with an answer from the Lieutenant-Governor to the Superintendent's wire, also a telegram for myself:

"Regina, 6th April. You are authorized to act for the Government in Indian matters in Treaty Number Seven in any way which you may deem advisable. E. Dewdney. Lieutenant-Governor, North-West Territory."

On the Indians being told, they expressed their pleasure by shaking hands all round. Their rations, I said, would be increased. I instructed Mr. Pocklington to raise the issue to one pound each of flour and beef per head daily. The previous rations had been half of this. I promised them seed grain and potatoes for their farming operations. I told them it was no fault of the Agent that their rations had been reduced and so placed him on a better footing with them, for which he afterwards thanked me. They promised to do as I advised and during the whole time of the rebellion no trouble whatever was caused by the Bloods. I visited them frequently during the summer, they continued quietly at work and that year raised good crops. I also visited the Piegans, increased their rations and settled a few minor grievances. Like the Bloods they gave us no trouble in that troubled period.

In May I drove to Blackfoot Crossing and found the Blackfeet more disturbed than any of the other tribes. They were nearer to the seat of the rebellion than the Bloods and Piegans. In consequence many rumours reached them. They were in the habit, too, of visiting Calgary where they heard plenty of mischievous tales circulated by parties trying to foment trouble. I increased the Indians' rations at this place and advised them to remain quiet. I made my headquarters at the Crossing with the Blackfeet during the summer, journeying to the other reserves at frequent intervals.

Although it has been stated in accounts of the behaviour of the Blackfeet during the rebellion that detachments of troops were quartered on their reserve, that they were visited by detachments of police, by Catholic priests and by various officials who collectively were supposed to have kept these Indians in subjection. There is no truth whatever in these statements. I was particularly careful to advise that none of the militia or police stationed at Calgary visit the reserve and none did so in consequence. I had given permission on several occasions to Indians to visit Calgary, generally with a written permit. But the Blackfeet, many without permits, travelled back and forth as was their custom. These visits occasioned much unnecessary alarm, adding to the apprehension of Calgary's population caused by rumours of impending outbreaks among the southern Indians.

On 6th July I received a letter from Father Lacombe at Calgary, who had not visited the Blackfeet during the summer. Here is a portion:

"Dear Captain Denny,

"The people of Calgary are very uneasy at the presence of a large number of Blackfeet in the town. Would you be good enough to come up and take them away. They say you gave them permission to come and they will not leave without you tell them, so please come up as soon as you can."

I drove up the following day and sent the small party of Indians there, who were perfectly peaceable and much surprised at the excitement they created, back to the reserve. After this they followed my advise to remain quietly at home, since it was easily seen that these visits might lead to complications.

Since I was anxious for the Lieutenant-Governor to visit the Blackfeet, I wrote him stating that the Indians wished to see him and asked him to come. After being assured that they were perfectly peaceable and that he was in no danger, he decided to do so. He arrived in August. I met him with the chiefs and a large party of Indians at Gleichen station. He was rather taken aback at the sight of the crowd gathered to welcome him but drove with me out to the Blackfoot camp, where a very satisfactory interview took place. Endless promises were made by him for the future. Some were kept, others not.

On the Governor's return to Regina he forwarded the result of the interview to Prime Minister Macdonald at Ottawa, who sent me the following telegram to be read to Crowfoot and the Blackfoot nation:

Imasees, Chief Big Bear's second son, was the instigator of the Rebellion's only atrocity—the Frog Lake massacre. Afterwards, he escaped to the United States. He later returned, visiting Eastern Canada in war paint and feathers. Here he was feted by the politicians instead of being tried for murder.

Louis Riel, top right, was hanged for his part in the North-West Rebellion. As Imasees wasn't even charged for his role in the Frog Lake massacre, Riel's harsh sentence was considered by many to be a miscarriage of justice.

Seven of the nine men murdered at Frog Lake, and NWMP Constable Cowan, killed and mutilated at Fort Pitt, are today buried in Frog Lake Historic Park.

"The good words of Crowfoot are appreciated by the Big Chief at Ottawa. The loyalty of the Blackfeet will never be forgotten. Crowfoot's words shall be sent to the Queen. All Mr. Dewdney's promises shall be faithfully carried out."

Care was necessary in handling the southern Indians at this time, with outside interference increasing the difficulties, especially when such instructions as the following, wired in cipher, were received:

"Regina, 1st May.

"A few Crees some thirty in number around Cypress skulking. Would like Blackfeet to clean them out. Could this be done quietly? Advise me before taking action.

"E. Dewdney."

To this communication I replied:

"Blackfoot Crossing, 1st May.

"Will not send Blackfeet. Would all wish to start out. Could not keep track of them.

"C. E. Denny."

It can be seen from the foregoing that I had much to contend with this summer. I was kept busy while the rebellion lasted in combating ill-advised suggestions and keeping the Indians quiet on their reserves. The result of such action as advised would have taken all the able-bodied Indians out of Treaty Number Seven and started a nice little war to get them back again. I might relate several of these "wise" recommendations but the one will suffice.

Superintendent Cotton patrolled east from Fort Macleod towards the Cypress Hills during the summer and kept that section free from hostilities. Settlers in the south were not molested in any way.

When the rebellion ended with the capture of Riel and Big Bear all the militia stationed in the West were withdrawn. The men engaged in the militia received land grants of 160 acres on the conclusion of their terms of service. The Mounted Police received none. Thanks and promises were profuse after the rebellion. I received many such, being thanked with others by Sir John A. Macdonald in Parliament. I remained in charge of the treaty during the following winter, with the understanding that I should be appointed inspector of the treaty the following year. This promise was, however, never fulfilled.

In the spring of 1886 the Mounted Police were increased from 500 to 1,000 men. The increase was justified by the rush of population in the North-West after the Rebellion. Settlers flocked into the southern Alberta ranching country and into the farming country to the north and east, so that the duties of the force were much extended.

CHAPTER SEVENTEEN

Rapid Development in the North-West

In 1885 a massive round-up of some 60,000 cattle begins an era of wheat fields stretching over the horizon.

Telegraph lines were constructed in 1886 to many points such as Macleod, Lethbridge, Wood Mountain, and Edmonton not directly on the line of railroad. The whisky traffic increased considerably in the south during the rebellion as many points were unwatched and the people flocking into the country created a demand which could not easily be combated. Horse stealing had also become prevalent, many American Indians and white men making a business of it during the summer.

With the spread of population, the work of the Mounted Police underwent a change. Since the railroad now spanned the country and branch lines were in process of construction, good comfortable quarters were erected at different points for the police detachments. The long journeys of the past gave place to short patrols on which farms and ranches were visited and complaints promptly attended to. During the summer of 1884 some 2,000 settlers took up homesteads in Alberta. This was the beginning of the small farmer influx. From then on the leaseholder had gradually to give place to the settler class.

Difficulty arose between settlers and ranchers. Many squatted on leased land along the river fronts and shut off the watering places used by the range cattle. Some only took up land with the hope of being bought out by the ranch company on whose lease they planted themselves. Although bona-fide settlers were in the majority, much bad feeling was caused. It was natural, too, that the arriving farmer would look for the best location, one embracing a spring or a river flat. The friction spread until the Government appointed William Pearce to deal with the situation. He recommended that the small farmers should leave their gates open in the fall so that range cattle could gain access to the waterholes and shelter along the river bottoms. The farmers objected to this plan, claiming that their cattle would drift away with the range stock.

In 1885 the Government issued new regulations regarding leases and more encouragement was given to the settler. Homesteaders thereafter could take up land on any lease. Previously, it had been necessary to secure the permission of the leaseholder. No further leases of 21 years were to be granted and where possible existing leases of that length were to be cancelled.

The greatest and last general round-up in southern Alberta took place in May 1885. It was held at Fort Macleod and was attended by more than 100 men, with 15 chuckwagons and 500 horses, the captain being Jim Dunlap, foreman of the Cochrane Ranch. The country was covered from Pincher Creek nearly to the Cypress Hills and from Calgary south, about 60,000 head of cattle being gathered.

During the following winter, Jim Dunlap had the misfortune to freeze his feet while riding between Fort Macleod and the Cochrane ranch. Although every effort was made to save him, he eventually died from the effects. Dunlap came from Montana in charge of a drive of the first Cochrane cattle and was one of the best cattlemen in southern Alberta.

During the fall of this year great prairie fires swept the country both north and south. The Blackfoot reservation was burnt from end to end and most of the grass on the Military Colonization Ranch was destroyed. The Blackfeet, who had now begun to gather small herds of cattle, were much dissatisfied. They blamed the railroad, no doubt with justice, for causing these fires. From the earliest days prairie fires had been a scourge, giving much trouble to the police. With the influx of settlers they became more numerous and entailed much extra work.

Carelessness was often responsible. It was astonishing how fires once well started would travel and the distances they could jump with the wind behind them. Commissioner Herchmer reported an instance of fire crossing the Saskatchewan at Lime Lake, where it is 900 feet wide, as a result of lighted bark from a burning tree being carried over by the wind.

In the spring of 1887 William Pearce took a census of the cattle, horses, and sheep on the ranches south of Bow River and reported the number to the Government as being 104,000 head of cattle, 11,000 horses, and 24,000 sheep. The winter of 1886-7 was an unusually severe one and the loss in cattle was enormous. Stock drifted long distances and died by hundreds in the deep drifts in the coulees. Even the antelope perished in hundreds, often wandering into the settlements and being killed in the streets. At least 25,000 head of cattle were estimated to have died and in Montana losses were even greater.

The previous winter had been the mildest ever known and the ranchers had failed to put up sufficient hay. This severe winter was a costly lesson to the stockmen. From then on stock owners were careful to put up all the hay possible in such locations that it could be easily fed to cattle on the range during a hard winter.

The first agricultural fair in southern Alberta was held in October at Macleod and a private bank was opened at the same place. This institution charged three per cent per month for money loaned and was the cause of many a small rancher going bankrupt. The owner held mortgages on the property of many new settlers, who, being unable to pay the ruinous rate of interest, lost not only their farms but their stock. I remember the case of one man who had borrowed $600 from this bank, giving a mortgage not only on his homestead but on several lots in Macleod and 110 head of horses. Failing to pay the interest at the exorbitant rate, the mortgage was foreclosed and he lost everything. The banker afterwards sold the farm alone for $2,000. No wonder he quickly became rich.

Superintendent Crozier, who had been appointed Assistant Commissioner of the Mounted Police under Commissioner Irvine, left the force on the appointment of Lawrence Herchmer as the latter's successor. Superintendent Crozier was a most efficient officer. His dealings with the Sioux under Sitting Bull, his work during the rebellion and his success in all he undertook stamped him as one of the most capable men of the force. The commissionership was most certainly due him, not only for the services he had rendered but because he was next in seniority. His resignation on the position being given to an outsider was regretted by all his companions in the force.

During this period the work of the police was greatly increasing. There were constant patrols with settlers visited regularly and their complaints attended to. The police also had their hands full in trying to stamp out the increasing liquor traffic. Liquor arrived in a great variety of ways: alcohol as red ink; Jamaica ginger in sacks of oats; whisky in loads of hay; a hundred devices were used to evade the law. Horrible concoctions were invented by the smugglers to make quantity take the place of quality. Raw alcohol was usually imported and the trader, once it was safely cached in Alberta, proceeded to lengthen his stock by mixing it with water, bluestone, and tobacco. Instances of men being killed by the last draught from such kegs were not at all rare. Because prohibition was unpopular, the police received no assistance from the settlers in their endeavors to suppress the traffic. On the contrary, there was much opposition as the following notice in a Moosomin paper in 1883 testifies:

"Indignation meeting. — A meeting will be held in the Orange Hall to-morrow night to protest against the late mean and despicable action taken by the police in subpoenaing respectable and worthy citizens to give evidence as whisky sneaks, thus interfering with the liberty of freeborn subjects and as likely to intimidate good citizens from entering hotels. Every one should attend and protest against such a resurrected tombstone, ironheeled law, to bear which is to suffer worse than the slaves in Siberia. Arouse ye all."

One improvement was that the claims of the half-breeds, following the rebellion, received consideration at the hands of the Government. Patents for their farms were granted and other steps were taken to re-assure them as to their security of tenure. But the very nature of their mixed descent was bound to manifest itself in a spirit of unrest and a reluctance to adapt themselves to the new life forced upon them. In the old days, before the country had been invaded from the east, existence had been easy and pleasant.

Buffalo hunting, trapping, and trading with the Indians enabled them to live well and luxuriously. When the buffalo disappeared, they did very well at freighting. But this work ceased with the advent of the railroad and the old cart and pack trains were gradually abandoned. The half-breeds thus found their means of livelihood cut off. It was hoped they would settle down to farming, but the authorities were disappointed.

The Indians, being forced by circumstances to remain on their reserves, were gradually taking to farming and stock-raising. But there was considerable unrest among them for many years after the rebellion; in fact until the older generation, which had been used to the wild, free life of the early days, died out. Murders were committed and horse stealing and drunkenness were prevalent, giving an immense amount of work to the Mounted Police.

The enforcement of the Liquor Act was the greatest difficulty. Under cover of the permit system, by which citizens were allowed to have up to five gallons of liquor in their possession, much illicit liquor was run into the country. Few Indians were proof against the wiles of the whisky trader. One of these worthies had only to take a keg of spirits into camp to be sure of making a profitable sale. Many horses changed hands for it

5 30 AM
21 OCT

WISH YOU WERE HERE?

You or your friends can be! With Latebreaks you can spend a week at a fabulous Interval International resort at very special low rates. And best of all, you don't have to give up or exchange the weeks you own! Here's how:

CALL NOW 0181 336 9595

Here are some of the exciting destinations that you can go to right now:

Prices start from £90

Lanzarote	Austria Mts.	Atlantic City, NJ
Italy Coast	Malta	Margarita Island
Orlando, FL	Balearic Islands	Puerto Vallarta
Costa del Sol	Brazil	British Columbia
Tenerife	Argentina	Acapulco
Fuerteventura	Dominican Republic	Israel
Algarve, Portugal	Atlantic Coast/Florida	Aruba

Offer expires December 15, 1997

BUT HURRY! **Confirmations are made strictly on a first-come first-served basis!**

Interval International

All Latebreaks confirmations are final. Public and school holidays are generally not available and all offers include accommodations only. Accommodations will be booked no more than 59 days in advance.

#60394 u

U.S. POSTAGE
PAID
MIAMI. FL.
PERMIT NO 06633
ZIP CODE 33152
PAR AVION

U.S. POSTAGE
PAID
PERMIT NO. 7795

PRINTED MATTER

MAILED FROM ZIP CODE
OCT -7'97

INTERVAL INTERNATIONAL®
THE QUALITY HOLIDAY EXCHANGE NETWORK

Coombe Hill House, Beverley Way
London, SW20 0AR

Save an extra £15 off most Late Breaks. Upgrade to GoldCard membership 3 years only £84.00

7037326
DAVID & JUNE WALKER
64 BRAMLEY WAY
MAYLAND
CHELMSFORD EX CM3 0ET
GREAT BRITAIN

Once the railway arrived, so did settlers by the tens of thousands. Typical were Mr. and Mrs. Tom Ogden on their way to a homestead in Alberta.

and the Indian had to thank the trader's liquid goods for the trouble he brought on his neighbours and himself.

One cause of discontent among the Indians I have before mentioned. This was the ban against stolen property — horses — being brought into the Dominion. They did not so much object to being punished for stealing horses on the Canadian side of the border, but they felt it unjust to suffer for similar thefts from Americans, the more so since there still was no reciprocal provision south of the Line.

Taking it as a whole, however, the Indians were slowly making progress in the right direction. Many of the old men were dying off, but there was promise, supported in after years, that the oncoming generation would become self-supporting. It would have been unreasonable to expect, so short a time having elapsed since the plains Indians were wholly wild, that they would within a few years become as civilized as the white men who had supplanted them.

EPILOGUE:

As the author has described, by the 1890s the West had dramatically changed since the summer of 1874 when the fledgling North-West Mounted Police wended their slow way 800 miles westward. The millions of buffalo were gone, the Indians against their will had been herded onto reservations and the new Canadian Pacific Railway was bringing so many settlers that one Indian observed, "The plains are black with white men." As a result of this influx, Forts Calgary and Edmonton, along with other new communities which included Lethbridge near Fort Whoop-up, were beginning the growth that transformed them into cities.

As the Mounties in the 1870s had earned the respect of the Indians, so did they now win over the new arrivals. Most of them were totally inexperienced, on their isolated farms particularly vulnerable to the long winter with its sub-zero cold and enveloping blizzards.

To ensure their safety, in the late 1880s the NWMP established a network of police patrols that visited every settler. Patrols from Regina alone one year covered 350,000 miles, equivalent to five times around the earth — plus a side trip to the moon.

The lawmen carried out these duties under a totally unnecessary handicap — incredibly shabby treatment by Ottawa civil servants and politicians. The author has recounted his frustrations in dealing with the inept bureaucracy and lack of consideration for the welfare of the men. Nor was he alone. In 1874 the first Commissioner, George A. French, refused to make a new post at Swan River his headquarters because he felt that the barracks were unfit to live in. As a consequence of his continuing clash with politicians, he resigned two years later.

The Force's fourth Commissioner, L. W. Herchmer, was also appalled at the treatment of the men. Appointed in 1886, he noted with indignation: "The Indians at the Industrial School have beds! Yet the police, the finest body of men in the country, still sleep on boards and trestles."

In 1879 pay for a constable was cut from 75 cents a day to 40, and a free land grant of 160 acres on completion of enlistment was withdrawn. Then there was the frustration preceding the Riel Rebellion. It probably would never have occurred had the politicians listened to the policemen's warnings about unrest on the prairie. After the rebellion soldiers who had participated were awarded medals and a land grant. The policemen were ignored, even though members had been wounded or killed. Not until several years later was their excellent contribution acknowledged.

As the author has noted, policemen were sent on winter patrols without even a tent, and for many years the Indians and

In 1904 when the North-West Mounted Police became the Royal North-West Mounted Police, the useless pill-box hat had been replaced by the broad-brimmed cowboy style. It was worn officially for the first time at Queen Victoria's Diamond Jubilee in 1897, above.

In March 1969 a long-standing tradition which dated back to the force's birth in 1873 was broken when the last dog-team patrol took place. In 16 days Constable W. Townsend and Special Constable P. Benjamin made a 500-mile return journey through Arctic wilderness from Old Crow in the Yukon to the Mackenzie River.

whisky peddlars had better firearms. Food was generally substandard, the men revolting at Fort Macleod in 1883 because their food was bread, beef and tea three times a day, with the beef frequently bad. When their clothing wore out they had to buy their own, and not for 26 years was the ridiculous pill-box hat replaced by the sensible stetson. Constable Fred Bagley, the youngest member of the Force during the 1874 trek, recalled that not until 1897 were they issued butter — and it was rancid, bought from a man who just happened to have a warehouse full.

Despite such shabby treatment, the policemen maintained their high standard of public service. They would reaffirm this dedication to duty during the 1898 Klondike gold rush.

The force originally started policing the Yukon in 1895 when 19 men were sent to this northwest corner of Canada. They little realized that in three years there would be a stampede of 50,000 men to a little known river called the Klondike. When the rush broke out, reinforcements under Superintendent Sam Steele were sent north, although he had only 285 men to control the influx.

Since there was no food in the Yukon, Sam Steele decreed that every person had to bring one ton of supplies. The newcomers quickly learned that what Sam Steele said, he meant. At the summits of the White and Chilkoot Passes where snowfall is measured not in inches but in feet, each man was checked by NWMP officers.

When the ice left the Yukon River an armada of homespun craft embarked on the hazardous 550-mile journey downstream to the Klondike. Like the men who had populated the prairie, these gold-struck hopefuls were also inexperienced. For their own safety, Superintendent Steele ordered that each boat had to be inspected and registered. "Build them long, boys, and build them strong. The Yukon is both," was their advice. The lawmen checked over 7,000 of the home-made craft, saving many gold seekers from death in the Yukon's cold, white-water rapids.

In 1904 as a reward for dedicated service, King Edward VII decreed that the name of the force be changed to Royal North-West Mounted Police. Then in 1920 came another change and the frontier force passed into history — at least in name. To reflect that the men now served from the Atlantic to the Pacific and north to the entire Arctic, the force became the Royal Canadian Mounted Police.

But while the name was new, the force's heritage wasn't. It dated back to the early 1870s when Cecil Denny, Sam Steele, Fred Bagley and some 300 other red-jacketed and ill-equipped lawmen — only two of whom had police experience — headed West to uphold their shiny new motto, "Maintain the Right."

A selection of other HERITAGE HOUSE titles:

The PIONEER DAYS IN BRITISH COLUMBIA Series
Every article is true, many written or narrated by those who, 100 or more years ago, lived the experiences they relate. Each volume contains 160 pages in large format magazine size (8½ x 11), four-color covers, some 60,000 words of text and over 200 historical photos, many published for the first time.

A continuing Canadian best seller in three volumes which have sold over 75,000 copies. Each volume, $12.95

WHITE SLAVES OF THE NOOTKA
On March 22, 1803, while anchored in Nootka Sound on the West Coast of Vancouver Island, the *Boston* was attacked by "friendly" Nootka Indians. Twenty-five of her 27 crew were massacred, their heads "arranged in a line" for survivor John Jewitt to identify. Jewitt and another survivor became 2 of 50 slaves owned by Chief Maquina, never knowing what would come first ---- rescue or death.

The account of their ordeal, published in 1815, remains remarkably popular. New Western Canadian edition, well illustrated. 128 pages. $9.95

THE DEATH OF ALBERT JOHNSON: Mad Trapper of Rat River
Albert Johnson in 1932 triggered the greatest manhunt in Canada's Arctic history. In blizzards and numbing cold he was involved in four shoot-outs, killing one policeman and gravely wounding two other men before being shot to death.

This revised, enlarged edition includes photos taken by "Wop" May, the legendary bush pilot whose flying skill saved two lives during the manhunt. Another Canadian best seller. $7.95

OUTLAWS AND LAWMEN OF WESTERN CANADA
These true police cases prove that our history was anything but dull. Chapters in 160-page Volume Three, for instance, include Saskatchewan's Midnight Massacre, The Yukon's Christmas Day Assassins, When Guns Blazed at Banff, and Boone Helm — The Murdering Cannibal.

Each of the three volumes in this Canadian best seller series is well illustrated with maps and photos, with four-color photos on the covers. Volume One, $9.95; Volume Two, $8.95; Volume Three, $10.95

B.C. PROVINCIAL POLICE STORIES: Mystery and Murder from the Files of Western Canada's First Lawmen
The B.C. Police, born in 1858, were the first lawmen in Western Canada. During their 90 years of service they established a reputation as one of the most progressive police forces in North America. All cases in these best selling titles are reconstructed from archives and police files.
Volume One: 16 chapters, many photos, 128 pages. $9.95
Volume Two: 22 chapters, many photos, 144 pages. $9.95
Volume Three: 23 chapters, many photos, 160 pages. $12.95

B.C. BACKROADS
This best selling series contains complete information from Vancouver through the Fraser Canyon to Cache Creek, east to Kamloops country and north to the Cariboo. Also from Vancouver to Bridge River-Lillooet via Whistler. Each book contains mile-by-mile route mileage, history, fishing holes, wildlife, maps and photos.

Volume One — Garibaldi to Bridge River Country-Lillooet. $9.95
Volume Three — Junction Country: Boston Bar to Clinton. $9.95
Thompson-Cariboo: Highways, byways, backroads. $4.95

An Explorer's Guide: MARINE PARKS OF B.C.
To tens of thousands of boaters, B.C.'s Marine Parks are as welcome and convenient as their popular highway equivalents. This guide includes anchorages and onshore facilities, trails, picnic areas, campsites, history and other information. In addition, it is profusely illustrated with color and black and white photos, maps and charts.

Informative reading for boat owners from runabouts to cabin cruisers. 200 pages $12.95.

GO FISHING WITH THESE BEST SELLING TITLES

HOW TO CATCH SALMON — BASIC FUNDAMENTALS
The most popular salmon book ever written. Information on trolling, rigging tackle, most productive lures, proper depths, salmon habits, downriggers, where to find fish, and much more.

Sales over 130,000. 176 pages. $5.95

HOW TO CATCH SALMON — ADVANCED TECHNIQUES
The most comprehensive advanced salmon fishing book available. Over 200 pages crammed full of how-to-tips and easy-to-follow diagrams. Covers all popular salmon fishing methods: mooching, trolling with bait, spoons and plugs, catching giant chinook, and a creel full of other information.

A continuing best seller. 192 pages. $11.95

HOW TO CATCH CRABS: How popular is this book? This is the 11th printing, with sales over 90,000. $4.95

HOW TO CATCH BOTTOMFISH: Revised and expanded. $5.95

HOW TO CATCH SHELLFISH: Updated 4th printing.
144 pages. $3.95

HOW TO CATCH TROUT by Lee Straight, one of Canada's top outdoorsmen. 144 pages. $5.95

HOW TO COOK YOUR CATCH: Cooking seafood on the boat, in a camper or at the cabin. 8th printing. 192 pages. $4.95

FLY FISH THE TROUT LAKES
with Jack Shaw
Professional outdoor writers describe the author as a man "who can come away regularly with a string when everyone else has been skunked." In this book, he shares over 40 years of studying, raising and photographing all forms of lake insects and the behaviour of fish to them.

Written in an easy-to-follow style. 96 pages. $8.95

SALMON FISHING BRITISH COLUMBIA: Volumes One and Two
Since B.C. has some 7,000 miles of coastline, a problem to its 400,000 salmon anglers is where to fish. These books offer a solution. Volume One includes over 100 popular fishing holes around Vancouver Island. Volume Two covers the Mainland Coast from Vancouver to Jervis Inlet. Both include maps, gear to use, best times, lures and a tackle box full of other information.

Volume One — Vancouver Island. $9.95
Volume Two — Mainland Coast: Vancouver to Jervis Inlet. $11.95

Heritage House books are sold throughout Western Canada. If not available at your bookstore you may order direct from Heritage House, Unit 8, 17921 55 Ave., Surrey, B.C. V3S 6C4. Payment can be by cheque or money order but please add $1.00 a book to help pay postage and handling.
